CW01020625

Walking with Chiefs
Non-Fiction

First published in 2020 by Mellester Press

ISBN 978-0-473-52231-5 Hardcover
ISBN 978-0-473-52229-2 Softcover
ISBN 978-0-473-52230-8 Epub
ISBN 978-0-473-52232-2 Kindle

Published in New Zealand. A catalogue record of this
book is available from the National Library of New
Zealand.Kei te pātengi raraunga o Te Puna Mātauranga
o Aotearoa te whakarārangi o tēnei pukapuka.

With heart felt thanks.
Front cover image, Stephanie Huriana Fong (nee Martin)
Inside images by, Kendall Whanau
Anaru Ngawaka synopsis by Jaqi Brown

http://www.WalkingwithChiefs.com
Walking with Chiefs ©2020

Published by
Mellester Press 2020

Walking
With Chiefs

by
Ron Kendall

Published by
Mellester Press

Karakia (Prayer)

E Rangi, e Papa, e Te Whanau Atua

Whakatōhia to koutou manaakitanga

Ki roto i tēnei mahi o mātou

Sky Father and Earth Mother and

the family of gods, infuse your

blessings on this work of ours.

Contents

Dedicated to the Memory
of all our Tupuna

Foreword from the Author

'Remember who you are, and where you came from'

To many, this mantra may not evoke much of a reaction but to me it is a humble yet powerful statement not only for myself but for all Maori. To survive in this uncertain and sometimes crazy world that we live in I use this phrase to centre and ground myself as often as I need to.

These words allow me to honour, appreciate and show gratitude to all my Tupuna (Ancestors) who have gone before me and guided me to where I am today. These thoughts immerse my wairua (soul) in pride and a deep inner strength when I look back on the achievements of my ancestors and the legacy, they have left for us Maori as a people.

I had embarked on a spiritual journey a long time ago, even though at the beginning I was unaware that it had already begun. Standing here, I can now look back and acknowledge the very start of my journey and all the significant events or milestones that presented themselves along the way. It has taken a lot of faith and trust in what I was being shown to enable myself to continue my journey and along the way, there were many subsequent powerful visions in relation to lessons to be learnt. Some of these lessons were good and some were not so good but, in the end, they needed to happen in order that the full picture to be appreciated and understood. I found that patience is one of the most important aspects required for your journey, something I completely lacked at the start but with guidance and practice I now have an abundance of patience when it is required.

Time is an earthly advent and does not exist in the world of spirit. If you think things need to happen now because you are ready be prepared to be disappointed, be patient and learn to listen to your higher self. Learn to develop your own holistic outlook rather than focussing on things that only benefit yourself. You already have all the answers to all the questions you will ever have buried deep within yourself, you are just relearning how to access that information. Be patient, let go and trust that the universe and your guides are working with you to assist you in navigating your journey. Again, I give thanks to my creator and my Tupuna for their guidance and the patience they have allowed me to fully understand and comprehend these lessons.

Unfortunately, in my younger years I had hit so many brick walls when it came to be looking for answers or help to understand spiritual issues. Help or even understanding for that matter was never forthcoming from much of my family. In fact, the whole subject was treated with the same consideration as the plague. 'Don't talk about it' or 'you're being stupid' and 'You don't know what you are talking about' were just a few of the most common comments directed at me. Ridicule was one of the easiest ways for those concerned to try and make out that they were the centre of all knowledge and, to be honest, I just mentally cut them off and did not discuss these issues with them any further. In fact, it got to a stage that I was constantly anxious due to the visions I was seeing and ran from them on an almost daily basis. It even became so overwhelming that it was the primary reason Leanne and I left New Zealand. I had no other choice available to me at the time in order to address the constant inner conflict, confusion and anger. The visions were increasing in both frequency and intensity and with no support it was a very lonely existence. I felt that after so many years of feeling alone and isolated in dealing with what I was experiencing, I needed to get away from it. I can honestly say that if I had not made the break when I did, I do not think I would be here today as it was so difficult to deal with at a young age. I was told many years ago while trying to find help that people who dabble in this stuff and do not know what they are doing, can go mentally crazy. To be very honest, I know that before I left for Australia as a young man I was on the edge of the precipice. When you are constantly told not to speak to anyone about what you are going through you come to the realisation of just how isolated and lonely your life can really be and how bleak your outlook really seems.

After going down that road I would strongly recommend that if you find yourself in the same situation that I was in, disregard all the negative comments. Stand up and do not be afraid to go against what you have been taught and find someone you can talk to. Take the decision to find like-minded people and open up regardless of your upbringing or what those around you tell you is acceptable and what is not. Refuse to be oppressed and take that step for yourself, it is your journey alone. As difficult as it may seem to you, at times you will be required to turn your back on everything you think you know or what you have been taught. It may sound radical but believe me it is necessary in order to move forward or to fully comprehend what you are going through at the time. You will get used to it and it will get easier, it is just the process of breaking free of the constraints that keep you anchored to ego and allowing yourself to be set free. Your journey will be much more liberating and engaging when you disconnect from the directives and expectations of others and reconnect with your higher self.

There are many avenues available these days to connect with others on their own journey and the most important thing is just to stay open. In a way it works much like Bluetooth technology whereas if a number of devices have Bluetooth activated the devices recognise each other when in close proximity. Spirituality operates in much the same way. By learning to stay open you will recognise others that are open, and they will also recognise you. That is just how it works. When it first works for you, the realisation of what you have just achieved will serve as a reward for the work you have put in and more importantly you have taken one of the first steps in your personal journey. Be proud of what you have achieved and keep moving.

With what I call those terrible years behind me, I am now in a good place and enjoying life and all the lessons my Tupuna have taught me. I have been able to assist others on their journey as well as assist in correcting spiritual episodes being experienced by others which has allowed my knowledge to grow even more.

Hindsight is a beautiful thing in so much as I am now able to look back over a period of many years and see all the people who have come into my life and helped me, or ignited something within me which drove me to pursue this journey even though at times it was the last thing I wanted to do. I know now that people come into your life for a reason. For example, the reason my ex-wife Leanne entered my life was to help me to become aware of my spirituality, as well as getting me to take the biggest step in my life which went against everything I had ever known. Ultimately, she led me to someone who could help me to discover my key to the door of knowledge.

This instance served as an example to me for the future, as many times since I have had to walk away from everything I had known or been taught in order to move forward. That is a very big ask for some people who are so entrenched in where they are in life and they just cannot see why they need to set it to the side to move forward. Personally, to me that just illustrates that they are not 100 per cent ready for their journey. There is nothing wrong with that and it is by no means a negative, it just means the timing is not right but at some stage the timing will be right, and everything will fall into place. We are all different.

To my ex-wife for persevering with me I sincerely thank you Leanne as well as your mother Leonie for being so supportive, especially in the early years. Leonie was open and offered support in an understanding way in which I had never encountered before. Thank you, Leonie.

It was not until a significant event happened in my life that I was faced with a decision which only I could make. Based on an actual event at that time, I decided to accept the role prepared for me by embracing spirituality in order to protect my son.

Now that I look back, I can honestly say it was the best decision I made, and I have absolutely no regrets about making that decision. My journey has encountered many crossroads where I have been required to make an important decision, which was always mine to make. As I have journeyed along this path those decisions are much easier to make as I reconnect to my higher self, my past and my Tupuna. At quite a few vantage points of my journey when I looked back in order to go forward, I actually said to myself 'if I knew that this was what it was about all those years ago, I would have accepted it long ago'. I cannot tell you where your journey will take you as we all have our own set of lessons to learn. What I can tell you is that you are about to undertake the single most uplifting amazing experience you will undertake in this lifetime, bar none.

I had been asked to write a book by several people along the way after they had heard different parts of my story at different periods in my life. After quite a few years I finally did decide to write a book with the objective of assisting others to navigate their own spiritual journey. I discussed with my mother, several years before she passed away, my intention to write this book. She did not agree with me at first but when I told her I was going to do it anyway she came around to my way of thinking. I can honestly say I understood where mum was coming from due to her upbringing, but I believe that there are many like myself who are looking for help, or just the realisation that they are not the only ones in this situation.

I want to reach out to these souls to let them know that they are not alone and that we are all travelling in the same direction even though it may be by a different road.

A journey such as mine has no operating or user manual but you are driven to seek the answers you are looking for, even though you do not know where to find these answers or where the answers will lead you. I have had to learn to trust something that is not tangible or bought off the shelf as it were but more something, I can feel inside me and visualise by simply closing my eyes. Not something I would have thought that I would have been capable of as a young man, but I can honestly say that I now understand the true meaning of faith.

I never received any help in the early years, and I am hoping that by writing this book I can provide some assistance to those who are seeking answers but have nowhere to turn. Believe me, I know how that feels. The most important single piece of information I can share with you at this point is this. Do not be afraid to tell your story as it may be the key that unlocks someone else's prison and believe me at times when you have no one to talk to or seek help from, it does feel like a prison. Some of you may not be ready for such a journey but do not lose heart, it will all happen when the time is right. Do not try to force it, it does not work like that, just let go and trust.

While living in Perth I have been sought out by many people for spiritual guidance or house clearing and even one on one meditational training lessons. I have never advertised but people turn up on my doorstep after speaking with people I had helped previously, so I help where help is needed. These requests for help have even extended back to New Zealand on a number of occasions dealing with a range of instances which I have been able to resolve from here by utilising the skills I have acquired throughout this journey.

One of the most amazing things I have observed is that spirituality is universal and embraces pure love, compassion, empathy, consideration, respect, emotion and understanding. You do not have to be Maori to understand this story, our link with our past is unbroken, so we are still connected to our spiritual past and culture therefore allowing us to re-engage or encourage the spiritual side of Maori Culture.

Our culture has been accepted by our island nation of New Zealand as its national culture. In many ways we should give thanks for this as many other countries indigenous populations have feared much worse than we have in that respect, having just been pushed aside as if they never existed and disrespected at every turn. For this, I send light and love to our brothers and sisters, fellow spiritual guardians of our lands and all that is contained within and around them.

In accepting Maori Culture as New Zealand's national culture, it has allowed the Maori spiritual and cultural heritage to survive and thrive to a point where the new generation of Maori are embracing their heritage and culture, allowing it to grow much stronger than it was in my generation. In saying that, I have always referred to my generation as the lost generation. Our parents had a very difficult transition to the 'pakeha' way of life and were beaten at school for speaking their own language by their teachers and those in power. Do not get me wrong, I am not trying to racially slur our country's past. I have long forgiven the wrongs of the past on our people. Ultimately, resentment only harbours hatred and that is not what any of us want to portray.

The sad part of this story is that my parents, of my six brothers and four sisters and I took it upon themselves to withhold all knowledge of our culture, history and language from us as they believed this would protect us from being treated as they were. My own generation have now taken the mantle and are learning or have learnt Te Reo (language) and I have seen in many of them the first speck of light which shines within when about to embark on your own journey. I see that speck of light as a seed and part of my role is to encourage and assist with the growth of that light seed should the opportunity present itself. In order to not interfere with free will, this will only be facilitated if asked for and that is just how it works.

It has been this platform which has launched me on my journey and along the way I have discovered that spirituality is indeed global and other cultures all operate using the same template though we all alter it slightly to allow individual ownership. Kind of like the copyright law 10 percent change and you can claim ownership rule. We are not the only race capable of spirituality, we are one of many and in accepting our spirituality we become part of a universal family who embrace these ideologies.

My blood family is unique in that we are the result of combining the bloodline of two Rangatira (Chiefs) and Tohunga into one family line.

I am one of eleven children, who are the proud descendants of two noble northern Maori Rangatira (chief) and Tohunga, Atama Takaipaetu Paparangi (1814-1915) and Anaru Iehu Ngawaka (1872-1964). Anaru is actually the older brother of my great, great, great grandfather Parore Ngawaka who passed away in the Spanish flu epidemic which swept through New Zealand in 1918. It was said that Parore was sick and heard there were not enough able-bodied people left to bury the dead, so he walked six kms to his brother Anaru's house at Taieka on the shores of the Whangape Harbour which was being used as a Marae, Hospital and Morgue. There were 50 bodies lining the veranda when Parore arrived at the property where he sat down under a peach tree and succumbed to the influenza. After his death, Anaru took Parore's children under his wing and bought them up as his own. Parore's children all regarded Anaru as their grandfather after this and as such passed down the line as being our great, great, great, grandfather but in reality, he is our great, great, great, Uncle. Maori being Maori, we all remain attached to the umbilical cord of life that we know as whanau.

On the following pages, I have provided a synopsis of both lines of my whakapapa in an attempt to illustrate the prominence and powerful mana both men possessed in their own individual Hapu and Iwi. This in turn demonstrates the significance of merging both of these powerful spiritual energies into one bloodline which had been achieved by the union of Edwin Whitirua Kendall of Mitimiti and Kura Kendall (nee Ngawaka) originally of Whangape. My parents. Their legacy now continues on with their eleven children in this generation. It is a work in progress, but this account represents the start and continuation of my journey as a result of these two lineages' becoming combined.

Atama Takaipaetu Paparangi
Paramount Chief and Tohunga of Te Tao Maui Te Hapu Te Rarawa
Te Iwi Hokianga, subtribe of Ngapuhi, Mitimiti, Hokianga.
1814 -1915

Atama Takaipaetu Paparangi was born in the Hokianga Harbour district in 1814 and was the youngest son of Paparangi Paparangi, along with older siblings Rewi Paparangi and Huriana Paparangi.

According to Maori and tribal legend, the descendants of Atama migrated to Aotearoa aboard the Ngatokimatawhaorua and the Mamari well before the great migration. All of the whanau aboard both vessels were linked to Kupe the great navigator and discoverer who originally discovered Aotearoa, New Zealand.

The Ngatokimatawhaorua was commanded by Nukutawhiti the grandson of Kupe. aboard the re-adzed Matawhaorua which had sailed under the command of Kupe in the original voyage. Due to a powerful tapu placed on the vessel which did not allow food to be carried on board, a second Waka named Mamari also completed the journey to support Ngatokimatawhaorua.

Nukutawhiti, following detailed charts from Kupe's travels, navigated the waters known as Te Moana-nui-ā-Kiwa or the Pacific Ocean. The two Waka were guided to Aotearoa by two taniwha conjured up by Kupe to protect both vessels travelling back to Hokianga. Nukutawhiti landed his Waka on the north side of the Hokianga Harbour. The Waka Mamari whose commander was Ruanui, the brother in law of Nukutawhiti, landed on the south side of the Hokianga Harbour and settlements were established on both sides of the harbour. One of the two taniwha was sent back to Hawaiki to inform Kupe that both Waka had arrived in Aotearoha, while the other taniwha, Niniwa stands guard on the north side of the harbour along with Arai te Uru on the southern side. Arai te Uru was left by Kupe on his departure to guard Hokianga. The last resting place of Ngatokimatawhaorua is said to be in the Hokianga protected by tapu, though the exact location has been lost through the course of time.

Atama was the very last in the line of full-blooded ancestral Chiefs in the direct line of descendants linked to Kupe and the last in that same line of descendants to be adorned with a full facial moko. It is said that a young Atama fought against Hone Heke at Kororareka alongside Tamati Waka Nene in 1845. In later life as a result of embracing the Catholic faith he changed his name from Takaipaetu to Atama (Adam), while his wife changed her name to Ewa (Eve). He demanded total allegiance from his whanau, and everyone associated with Matihetihe Marae at Mitimiti to embrace Catholicism as their religious belief. He even went so far as to exhume any non-Catholics from the Urupa (cemetery) and rebury them in the surrounding mountains such was his commitment to Catholic faith. As a testament to the respect his people held for his power mana and ancestral lineage, the Mitimiti area remains a Catholic Community today. Atama Paparangi was known as a hard but fair man.

It was in 1901 during a royal visit by the Duke and Duchess of Cornwall that Atama met C.F. Goldie, a New Zealand artist who become synonymous with and an authority of paintings of Maori Chiefs and native persons of interest.

A close friendship developed between the two and in 1914 Goldie completed a portrait of Atama which is now housed at Auckland Museum. Atama became a favoured subject of Goldie and at six feet tall, with an intricate facial moko by the famous tattooist Huitara, he was considered a strikingly handsome figure. Throughout the 1930s Goldie submitted portraits of Atama to the Royal Academy, London and the Paris Salon.

After a long and eventful life Atama died at 100 years of age, immortalised by his friend C.F. Goldie.

Anaru Iehu Ngawaka, more popularly known as Naru or Andrew Ngawaka, was born in the Whangape area of north Hokianga, in 1872. His father, Iehu Ngawaka, a farmer, and his mother, Nganeko Murray, also known as Mary Ngahemo Ngawaka of Te Aupouri/ Te Rarawa Iwi. He had a younger brother Parore Ngawaka who married Ani Te Paa from Ahipara and had three children. Parore died as a result of the influenza epidemic that ravaged New Zealand during the first world war. As a result, Naru stepped into help raise Parore's children, Miha Thomas (Bailey) Tare (Dolly) and Thomas my grandfather whose war records state his birth as 1st March 1903 and he served in both the first and second world wars, he passed away 2nd May 1965.

Anaru Iehu Ngawaka
1872–1964
Rangatira, Tohunga and Anglican Clergyman of Whangape, Northland, NZ
Te Tawhiu te Hapu, Te Rarawa Te Iwi, subtribe of Ngapuhi,
Whangape, Northern Hokianga

Anaru Iehu Ngawaka, more popularly known as Naru or Andrew Ngawaka, was born in the Whangape area of north Hokianga, in 1872. His father, Iehu Ngawaka, a farmer, and his mother, Nganeko Murray, also known as Mary Ngahemo Ngawaka of Te Aupouri/ Te Rarawa Iwi. He had a younger brother Parore Ngawaka who married Ani Te Paa from Ahipara and had three children. Parore died as a result of the influenza epidemic that ravaged New Zealand during the first world war. As a result, Naru stepped into help raise Parore's children, Miha Thomas (Bailey) Tare (Dolly) and Thomas my grandfather whose war records state his birth as 1st March 1903 and he served in both the first and second world wars, he passed away 2nd May 1965).

Naru was a descendant of Nukutawhiti and Ruanui of the Ngatokimatawhaorua and Mamari canoes respectively. His ancestry connected him to many Northland tribes, including Ngapuhi and Te Aupouri, but he was principally of Te Rarawa and was a direct descendant of Tarutaru and Ruapounamu. His first marriage was to Maraea Wetini of Ngati Whatua, whose father was Hori Wetini and mother Mihiwera Paikea. They were married at Wharerimu, Pawarenga. They had eight children.With other elders and rangatira of Ngati Haua, Naru and his father supported education for the children and assisted with the introduction of formal schooling in the Whangape area. They offered land for the school and buildings and helped in their ongoing upkeep.

Naru's public debates on the Marae at Waitangi with Apirana Ngata over Treaty of Waitangi issues are legendary. His commitment to the upholding of the 1835 Declaration of the Independence of New Zealand and of the treaty had been instilled in him by his father and ancestors. He was a direct descendant of signatories to both documents, namely Papahia and Te Huhu of Whangape and Nopera Pana-kareao of Kaitaia. Occasionally, he appeared as an expert witness on land claims, and invoked Maori rights and obligations under the treaty.

Under the influence of the Reverend Hone Tana Papahia, Naru was considered for ordination to the Anglican priesthood. He became the first Maori to be ordained deacon without first going to St John College in Auckland. The ceremony took place on 12 May 1940 at Otiria Marae, Moerewa. He was in his late 60s at the time. Frederick Bennett, Anglican bishop of Aotearoa, conducted the service and had persuaded the bishop of Auckland, W. J. Simkin, that the ordination should go ahead. Naru was licensed to minister in the Maori district of Whangape. Simkin did not, however approve full ordination as a priest. He could not reconcile his views on what he considered to be tohungaism with the Christian priesthood. Naru had no such conflict and practiced both Maori and Anglican forms of ministry, including healing. He travelled throughout New Zealand. Naru Ngawaka died at Whangape on 15 August 1964 and was buried there. He was survived by Ngahiraka Raroa, and two daughters and two sons from his first marriage to Maraea Wetini.

Naru was an acknowledged authority on whakapapa, Maori custom, illness (healer) and sacred places, the Treaty of Waitangi, and the Bible. He gained a reputation as a brilliant speaker and preacher in both Maori and English. His ability to heal and his gift of foresight are said to have come from his ancestors Tiari and Iehu. An advocate for the effective use of Maori land, he gained prominence as a champion of Maori rights under the Treaty of Waitangi. Like Ngata, Peter Buck, Te Puea Herangi and Whina Cooper, he was one of the new generations of Maori leaders serving and leading their people into the twentieth century.

Anaru Ngawaka's Homestead at Taieka, Whangape
Northland New Zealand on the shores of Whangape Harbour

This is my story on how I reclaimed my spirituality with the patience and dedication of my great, great, great, grandfather Atama Paparangi, my father Edwin Whitirua Kendall and my great Uncle Tom Walsh. My great, great, grandfather Anaru Ngawaka has always been behind me throughout this journey but I had to make a choice as to which Rangatira would teach me and I had chosen Atama Paparangi as my mentor. I hope my story gives you an insight to any questions you may have had regarding spirituality and releases you from the current bonds of a busy hectic life to one which embraces peace, love, empathy, compassion, tolerance and understanding.

This book is my account of how my journey has transpired over the past 47 years and I hope you are able to draw from my experiences to help you along the way or just to understand and know that you are not alone. We are many and you need to know we are here for you. We all have a way of turning up when you least expect it, but it will always be when you need us. Once you are reconnected, you will be more aware of how this works as you will also adapt to your role in conjunction with other like-minded souls.

My journey has allowed me to rediscover my higher self and introduced me to the most amazing helpers you will ever need, the travellers. The travellers are individuals who are on their own journey but we randomly cross paths then recognise each other as travellers so we exchange information in order to help each other to move forward. We are all drawn to and recognise each other by many methods. It can be as simple as a single word or a phrase that allows you to recognise a traveller, you will just know. Dialogue will quickly follow and then the floodgates will burst open with information. Again, the raw emotion, feelings and energy you experience in these transactions is nothing short of amazing and an experience that I would describe as being almost addictive.

On many occasions it was I who had information for others and to this day this seems to be the norm, although earlier on it was I that was receiving information. Along the way I began to see that all these people had one thing in common with me, we were all searching for answers. Although we may not have been at the same level at the time of our meeting, the information I gave them or that they gave me was what was needed by each of us at that time for the crossroad that we were facing. Once you have learnt to stay open you will also be a traveller as I am. During my journey I assist others to expand their consciousness or they help me to expand mine. Again, these are some of the secrets revealed to me by my Tupuna (Ancestors).

Spirituality is available to everyone, we were all born with it. Ultimately, we are all spiritual beings here to learn from a human experience. Along the way, with our lives getting so busy we seem to have lost the path or focus and have replaced it with such things as career, busy lifestyles, ego, partner's, family, work etc. These are just some of the requirements we place upon ourselves relating to meeting the demanding daily expectations of life. The world today has a vast array of distractions compared to back in my grandparents' time and even my parents time for that matter. I believe Maori of old, meaning generations ago, were far more spiritual than we are today just because it was a different time and place. Many of today's life distractions were non-existent back in their time, so it was easier to practice and socially and tribally accepted as far as spirituality goes.

When I think back to the time of my grandparents' and my parent's, they witnessed so many changes in their world during their lifetimes. For my grandparents' they experienced the colonialisation of their lands, steam engines, world wars and the degradation of their culture among many others. For my parent's, they experienced a world war, the changing of the New Zealand landscape as far as our culture is concerned, racism, motor cars and even putting a man on the moon just to name a few. In both cases these examples merely scratch the surface of the massive changes they were subjected to as far as the world was concerned and what was happening in New Zealand. We are all very capable of reclaiming our spiritual birth right; all that is required is some commitment and taking the initiative to ask for it. It is your choice. Choice being the first of the three C's.

You must first make the Choice to take a
Chance in order to create Change.

I feel this statement is very poignant to my journey as you will be tasked with making choices on many occasions. My whole journey has been about me making the choice to continue or stop my journey, do or do not do the task in front of me, take the next step that I need to take or not. It is all reliant on your belief in yourself, your faith and the knowledge that what you are doing is what you need to do because it is right for you, right for your journey and right for your own spiritual growth. You will just know if it is right for you. Your very being will give you signals that you will not miss.

One thing you should consider while reading this book is that there are a thousand roads to get to your destination. This was my path. Your path may not necessarily be the same. We all have different paths so do not lose heart. It is ok to take your own path. Just have faith that you are on the journey that you are meant to be on. Own it. The universe has a way of making things work out the way they are supposed to and will also ensure everything you need to learn is presented during your journey. The choice then is yours. It is your choice whether you take the next step or not. Remember that your journey is a journey to self, to reconnect with your higher self. It will require that you strip off all the armour you have accumulated over the years to protect yourself in order that you can really see who you are, so you can see the real you. At times it may make you feel vulnerable, but it is at these times you have the most to gain from your experiences.

Let go of fear, there is nothing to fear but fear itself. Let go of ego as it serves no purpose to you on your journey and embrace all-encompassing love or aroha. Many will find it difficult to let go of all they know in order to embrace what you need to learn but rest assured, you can always pick it up again after each of your sessions.

Spirituality is a journey within. There are many facets which relate directly to your journey that you will only discover by going within, so go forward in the knowledge that you already know the answers, you are just reconnecting in much the same way that you would reconnect your computer to your modem. If you keep it simple, believe it or not it will be simple.

If you have found this book, it was written for you. It was written because someone other than yourself has stood in the precise place you are standing in right now, looking for the very same answers you are seeking, feeling isolated and feeling different to everyone else, being ridiculed by others who don't have the courage to face their own fears or are just not ready to undertake their own journey. That person was me. Please feel free to take what you need from this book to help you move along from the current point in your journey. Feel free to use it as often as you need as it may assist you in getting to where you need to get to on your journey. There are no wrong pathways on your journey just deviations. By reconnecting with your higher self your body will let you know when you have deviated off the main path which will allow you to correct your course.

The important thing here to acknowledge is the need to continually acquire and maintain balance. I have found that balance is the key to your own inner harmony which in return allows you to expand your consciousness at a rapid rate. There are other common examples of this balance which you would have already heard of, such as Yin and Yang, good versus evil, left and right, up and down. They all represent opposing forces that when in sync create balance.

There is a very fine line down the centre of these opposing forces which represents balance. Your spiritual journey is a lesson in finding that fine line and making it your own. This is your own personal path to enlightenment. Obviously, there are ramifications should you swerve off centre, but this can be corrected by realigning the nature of your intent. The nature of your intent will determine which road you will travel so be sure to choose wisely. You will learn these lessons and more along the way.

Learn to love yourself (not in a vain way) Have Trust, have faith and let go.

Again, if you have found this book, you are ready for it. Sit back, take a deep breath, relax, and welcome to my journey.

Walk in Love and Light
Ron

'Be still and quieten all the noise in your mind, because, if the sound of your own voice is the only thing you hear.........you aren't learning anything.'

Ron Kendall

CHAPTER 1

Growing Pains

I was born into a family of eleven children four girls and seven boys. My early years were spent in the small town of Pukekohe in South Auckland, New Zealand. Well it was small back then. I had what I thought was a normal early childhood with schooling and sports teams etc. and from what I remember it was an enjoyable childhood.

This time in New Zealand history was volatile due to racial tensions in Pukekohe at the time between Maori and Pakeha (white people). To be honest, I cannot say I took too much notice of this at the time as I just thought it was the norm and I was way too busy having fun with my mates, many of whom were pakeha as well as Maori. I still maintain contact with many of them today.

I remember all the times we worked on market gardens as small kids with mum clipping and picking onions and picking potatoes. There were long rows of spuds and onions and there was also the heartbreak of working yourself up over a rise to see the same row keep going out of sight. For us young kids it was heart-breaking but to our mother it was just another day at work. She could outwork most men our mother. She was born and raised in a place called Whangape and by all accounts had a very hard upbringing. This was obviously where she gained her no nonsense go hard work ethic. Even though we all hated working in the gardens I still look back on those times and think to myself, overall it was a pretty good childhood. I think that we all gave mum a lot of respect for being such a hard worker.

We were not the only ones either. Some of our friend's families, all Maori of course, would also be working the market gardens alongside us. Funnily enough I recently saw a documentary on Maori TV programme Te Karere about the racism in Pukekohe in the fifties and sixties. Tini Astle was interviewed for the story and I remember her and her boys also on the market gardens when I was very young. She said that she had seen how racism was back in those times in America and other places around the world and realised we had the same thing here. I was born in 1965 so as a young kid back then it did not even register with me but now when I look back, I can understand and agree with her comparison.

For example, I have many friends and family who are right into reggae music and I asked quite a few of them in the past what they liked about it. On almost every occasion their answer was that the music talked about their struggle and oppression as poor people of coloured skin. My response had always been to look at the struggle and oppression of your own people. We Maori have had to rise against the same struggles as have every other coloured race in the world. This again brings us back to the first sentence of this book. *Remember who you are and where you come from.* This simple sentence allows us all to come together as a people not as individuals and gives us inner strength with which we can stand together to action change. This statement is not only my opinion but one which has been forged through the teachings of my guides and my Tupuna.

On several occasions, (when I was very young) I remember us all as a family sitting around the dinner table and the topic of racism would come up. I remember thinking to myself, wow, I must have slept through that part. Life for me was as it should be at that stage….it was a kid's life. At that time dad was also one of the Maori wardens in town and we started holding discos at the Catholic Hall every second week to help keep Maori youth off the streets. Some of the kids both Maori and Pakeha would turn up with no money and mum would get them to help setup and pack up. They would be let in for free and they would get a good kai of whatever mum cooked up in her massive boil-up pots, complete with fried bread. These kids would have a good time and then help us pack up at the end of the night.

I can still remember all the holidays and trips we would take to Kaiaua, Kariotahi, Big Bay and Hot Water Beach, to name a few. We would all pile into the van then when we got older the oldest siblings would take their cars and friends used to come in their own cars as well. Great days for sure. With friends tagging along our large family got to be an even bigger extended family. Again, many of those friendships have stood the test of time and are as strong as ever today between us siblings and our childhood friends.

We also had many cousins around the South Auckland area and at times they would come with us on holidays or we would have a huge family get together and have a ball. It was a great way to keep in touch but an even better way to spend the holidays.

There were times when we would all be around the table at home having had dinner when mum and dad would talk about the farm. Being so young I used to take it all in but really, I never knew where the farm was. The story was that we had moved to Pukekohe so that we kids could get a better education and the farm had been leased out. I was not even born at that time and considering my place in the family, I had not even been considered back then, but the older siblings remembered. The Mitimiti farm had been in the family for generations and is in the far north of New Zealand on the west coast. It is in an area known as Hokianga and in a part of Northland considered by many to be the birthplace of New Zealand. Mitimiti is said to be one of the last places Maori spirits stop to drink from the Mitimiti stream on their way north to Cape Reinga before heading back to the ancestral lands of Hawaiki.

Hokianga Harbour is where Kupe landed when he discovered New Zealand in his Waka (sea faring canoe) named Matawhaorua. After exploring the whole of New Zealand, he once again set sail from Hokianga and travelled back to Hawaiki. Years after his return to Hawaiki, his Waka was re-adzed and re named Ngatokimatawhaorua after the original Waka before his descendant's Nukutawhiti and Ruanui returned to Hokianga from Hawaiki guided by detailed charts left by Kupe and powerful karakia.

The Hokianga almost became the capital of New Zealand back in the early days of colonisation. Rawene was mooted as being the new capital as all the kauri logging was being carried out in the

Hokianga back in the day. The new capital eventually became the Bay of Islands and later Auckland before finally being moved to Wellington. The history of the kauri logging can be viewed at many of the small tourist attractions right through the Hokianga.

I made many good friends in my early years in Pukekohe, Mitimiti and Panguru. Many of those friendships have weathered the years and when I do go home and catch up with many of these old friends it is as if we had never been apart.

I have been away from New Zealand now for roughly 34 years and what really stands out to me is that quite a few of those friends from those towns are in Perth. The ones that are not in Perth I have been able to reconnect with on Facebook so in reality the whole support network of friends and whanau I had as a young man, I now have again.

This has been my strength over the past twenty years or so, as my journey has sometimes worn me down so the ability to catch up online with some of these people makes me feel reenergised and ready to do it all over again. During your journey you may feel a bit isolated and lonely, but it is all part of the process. In the early days I felt the loneliness, whereas these days I find peace in solitude. The lesson is to find comfort in solitude and not despair.

There is a lesson in everything you experience on your journey. If the outcome of the lesson seems harsh or brutal, do not take it personally, you are better than that, just be sure to look for the lesson and you will find it. You will find, as I did, that on occasion the way some of the lessons are delivered from your guides are very powerful and some may even seem to be soul-destroying. I use this term because I have been on the receiving end of a few of these lessons. Do not take it personally, it is in no way a reflection on you in any way shape or form. The lessons are brutally honest and direct, but they honestly hold no malice or ill will toward you at all, they are just delivered in such a way that you cannot mistake what it is that you are being taught. I find that these lessons are significant in what they are portraying but more importantly, I have never forgotten those lessons. Unlike our mothers our guides will not continually repeat themselves or re phrase the message to spare your feelings. The message is relayed in such a way that you do not misinterpret or forget what has been divulged.

I did not have anyone to let me know the little secrets along the way. Instead I would beat myself up allowing my very essence to be crushed on numerous occasions before I understood how it all worked. I just kept getting back up because by this stage, I knew I was meant to learn this stuff. I lost a lot of time in these instances as it could take me a couple of weeks to pick myself up, dust myself off and recover from some of these lessons. Once I knew to accept the lesson for what it was without taking anything personally, the lessons were a lot easier.

I know that there will be many walking a similar path to the one I am walking and have subconsciously noticed a monumental shift in consciousness in the last decade as a result of more people awakening from their slumber and seeking out the answers to their questions. I have already met a few of them and it is for this reason that I want to pass on some of my insights in order that they will assist others on their journey. I will not divulge the majority of the lessons that I mastered but rather just bits and pieces. Those lessons were for me but yours may be different. Do not be disheartened if you take a different path to mine. If in doubt, just tell yourself *'All roads lead to Rome'* because that is the truth of it. This is your journey, yours to own and complete. What you require to complete your journey will be presented to you.

Walk in peace and light.

CHAPTER 2

Awakening from My Slumber

I can still vividly remember the night mum and dad told us we would be heading up north to the farm for a holiday. We were sitting around the dinner table when they told us younger kids. I was excited as, asking a thousand different dumb questions as you do and being told if I don't stop the questions I will not be going.

We were going up to the farm for the Easter break. The year was 1973 and I was 7 years old. I would be 8 in November. Most of us kids were born in Pukekohe while some of the eldest siblings were born in Rawene, the closest hospital to the farm. I knew nothing of the place, but the older siblings said they still had some vague memories of the farm. I was just excited to be going somewhere new but knew nothing about the place we would be visiting let alone where it was.

Dad had hired two cars to go on the trip, an orange Ford Falcon 500 station wagon and a white/ crème mini clubman, to get us all up there safely. I was full of excitement and could not wait to go. The early part of the week seemed to drag as I just could not wait to be going to the farm. To be honest, up until this point in time I did not really know that there was a farm, even though it had been spoken about several times. We were going and it finally sunk into me that we did have a farm. It was getting harder to sleep at night the closer we got to leaving.

We packed up both cars and headed off on the Thursday afternoon. The roads were so busy that when it got dark, all you could see were headlights for miles coming toward you and red tail lights for miles in front of you. The roads into the north were nowhere as good as they are today with the old roads going up east coast bays through to Orewa / Waiwera and on. I loved the coastal views going through these areas. There was no motorway and tunnel back then and there were still toll booths on the Auckland Harbour Bridge.

We had to make several stops on the way for toilet stops and a brother's car sickness but once we arrived in Whangarei, we stopped in at Kamo to a takeaway bar for something to eat. After eating we set off north again and found the traffic was not as heavy as it was on the south side of the city as we continued travelling into the night further and further north. We arrived at Mitimiti in the early hours of the morning.

Upon arrival we got out of the car and was greeted by a brisk and cool southerly wind and the sound of wild rolling ocean surf. The breeze and the sound of the wild surf felt overwhelming at first but after a few minutes it felt very soothing and welcoming. There were no streetlights here so there was no light pollution to give you any idea of your surroundings in the dark but when you looked up, the view of the Milky Way was unbelievably amazing. I have on many occasions since just lay down on the grass at night staring into the Milky Way and being overwhelmed by the view. It is not until you see the night sky in this way that you truly appreciate the absolute beauty of the universe.

We met our Uncle and Aunty who stayed in the old homestead and were given some kai (food) and then quickly ushered off to bed while the elders continued talking in the kitchen. We had to unload the station wagon and then the three of us younger boys slept in a bed made in the back with the seats folded down. We thought it was awesome. It had been a long trip and sleep came easy for us.

The old Kendall Homestead, Mitimiti, Northland New Zealand

The next morning, I woke up early still excited by our new surroundings. It was daylight but the sun was still being hidden by the rugged steep mountains. As I peered out the car window, I thought it really weird because as I looked up at the mountains it reminded me of the start of the show M*A*S*H, and I was expecting an army helicopter to come over the top of the mountains at any minute. I woke my younger brother Mal and told him about the view, and we both laughed. I got out of the car and walked around.

I was in awe of the beauty I was witnessing, look to the east and see mountains high and proud, then turn and look west and you have 180-degree uninterrupted views of the Tasman Sea with its big rolling surf.

Again, the rolling surf and the continuous roar of the crashing waves were just so soothing to me. I felt a very warm feeling come over me, even though there was a brisk southerly wind blowing. I still get that feeling to this day every time I go home. It is a very special place to me. I thought to myself then what a beautiful place this is and since then its natural beauty never ceases to amaze me. The pure beauty of the place with its endless white sand beaches, rolling thunderous waves and mountainous terrain has you taking a deep breath and you cannot help but admire what nature has conjured up for us to enjoy.

The next few days were awesome. We met our cousins who also lived in the homestead at the time and the routine was easy; get up, have breakfast, do the dishes, clean the house, make the beds, then off to explore everything we could fit in.

We were introduced to other cousins from the area, taught to ride horses on the beach, gather seafood, go fishing and go trekking up the mountains to waterfalls or high ridges as well as pick Lupin seeds. We all had a great time. It was days like this that you wished the days would never end. I developed an instant infinity for the place as everyone else did and just enjoyed all there was to enjoy while we were there.

What I did not know was that I was soon to be introduced to

something completely foreign to me in the early hours on Sunday morning, something that began my personal spiritual journey even though I did not know it at the time.

Saturday arrived and as normal the same routine was followed with the difference that our bedding from the station wagon was bought inside the lounge room. The lounge room was very large with an impressive large ornate kauri fireplace and high solid kauri carved ceilings. We were told that back in the early days prior to there being a Marae in the area, the deceased would lay in state here prior to the funeral service. As is Maori custom, they would lay in state for three days.

Anyway, we set up our bedding and that evening the adults went off to the hotel 30 kms away in Kohukohu. The older teenagers were left in charge of us young ones and we watched a movie before heading to bed. I woke in the early hours of the morning, maybe 1 or 2 am, and needed to go to the toilet. This was located outside alongside the laundry, so I got up and went out passing through the kitchen, the adults were back and had a guitar playing party songs and having a good time.

I went outside where there was an old armchair on the porch. I saw an old man sitting there and began talking with him. We chatted for a while, exchanging small talk, he wanted to know who I was, and then I proceeded to the toilet. When I returned, he was still there so we chatted some more. We had just finished talking and as I turned and put my hand on the door handle, my father opened the door from inside, looked at me and asked who I was talking to.

I answered 'just talking to this old man dad' but when I turned to show him, the man was no longer there. I just went inside and went to bed not thinking anything of it. The next morning at breakfast dad asked me if I was ok. I just said yeah and left it there. After breakfast, the sisters were looking at the family pictures all through the lounge. This was the family wall which had photos from way back of relatives at family gatherings and such. I looked through all the frames and remember feeling a very strong warm and welcoming sensation. It was not until much later in life that I could relate those feelings from that initial visit to Mitimiti, to having both our Tupuna under the one roof. The Ngawaka, or Whangape Tupuna were represented in the homestead by the Murray family from Whangape who were working the farm, and our Tupuna were represented by my family even if we were only visiting at the time.

The previous night was the first time I had seen, and unbeknown to me, my awakening had begun. It would take many more years for me to stir and respond but looking back this was most definitely the first step.

We began visiting Mitimiti on every holiday and long weekend from here on in as the bond with my heritage and culture slowly began to take shape and come alive.

I did not realise it at the time, but a small fire had been ignited within me which allowed me to draw on an energy which until this point of my life, I never knew existed. Being young, I just accepted it as being the norm and took it all in as I needed it.

As I found out later in life, this ability would indeed be an asset to me for the duration of my journey.

For the next year or so I never experienced anything out of the norm but inside, deep in my core, I could feel changes taking place within. These changes included visions or dreams resulting in confusion and anger. I think the anger came from trying to find answers by asking questions and being told I was silly, going crazy or did not know what I was talking about and the confusion was because nothing was forthcoming as I did not understand what I was seeing or what it meant.

Because of this, I just withdrew and stayed closed to what I considered to be outsiders. As I grew older, it came to include anyone who ridiculed me for bringing it up, sadly, even some of my own family members.

From where I stood when I was being trained, I looked back on the judgements of others during my lifetime who found more entertainment in ridiculing or judging me for my actions. I could see that not everyone had started their journey, so armed with that knowledge I went and looked inside of myself to find love from within to forgive them.

In order to travel light on your journey, forgiveness is the best way to achieve this. You are not doing it for their benefit you are doing it for your own benefit, to give you peace. Letting go of anger is the most productive way to work your way through this life but with all of life's trials and tribulations it can sometimes prove to be a lot easier to say than do but you will find it is a facet of your journey that you will need to come to terms with as quickly as you can.

It was not until several years later that the next memory of significance took place. I was 11 years old at this stage.

My grandmother on my mother's side had been diagnosed with cancer and was being cared for by our Aunty Martha in Mangere. I remember nanna as a gentle old lady who always had a kind word for us. As is the case with all kids, I loved my nanna.

We went up to visit nanna most Sundays along with other relatives and would hold karakia (prayers) for her and then share a meal. Us kids would play while the adults discussed what was needed for the following weeks care for our nanna, or just generally catching up.

It was on the last visit I had with nan prior to her passing that something else happened. On this occasion I remember a bunch of us kids walking into her room and she reached her hand out to me making a big fuss over me telling me I was growing into a fine young man.

We all said hello and kissed her on the cheek and after a little while she asked us all to leave the room. We thought she was tired, so we all started walking out, but she reached out and said to me 'not you boy, you stay here a while'.

I really thought I was in trouble and walked over to her bed expecting to be told off for something. She told me to close the door, which I did. I walked back to the side of her bed and she once again grabbed my hand and told me what I fine young man I was growing up to be.

Suddenly she went quiet, then said to me 'you need to prepare yourself boy, you are the one'. I had no idea what she was talking about, so I just nodded and said yes nanna. She told me again as if to clarify what she had said, and again I said yes nanna and nodded. She closed her eyes and said I am tired now boy, so I kissed her again on the cheek and left the room. That was the last time I saw my nanna alive.

The following Wednesday I was at school at Pukekohe Intermediate School. It was a nice sunny day. I remember it well. I was on gate patrol during the lunch break, you know the deal, if you have a gate pass you can leave the school grounds if not, then you cannot. I can vividly remember the day because the gates I was stationed at were on the top tennis courts and normally I would be up there playing tennis with my mates. They were playing tennis and I was on gate duty. I was thinking to myself man I wish I did not have to do this, it's a choice day for playing tennis. Yep, I was a typical teenager, always complaining.

At just prior to 1 o'clock, I know the time because I had just signed a gate pass and put the time on it, I saw a mini whirlwind come up the side of the bank from the teacher's carpark and start to move around the tennis courts. The kids playing tennis all stopped playing and we all watched it dancing around the court. There was dust and leaves being whipped up by the wind and it looked awesome. It moved over toward me then suddenly I was in the centre of it as it stopped and just swirled around me. It felt so warm and powerful yet so serene and peaceful

I do not know how long it went on for, 30 seconds a minute maybe, before it moved along and then just as fast as it came it disappeared.

My friends all rushed over to see if I was ok as they saw what happened. I just told them I was ok and left it at that. I did not elaborate on what I had experienced, and I am not sure if it was because I feared being ridiculed again, or because I just took it, accepted it and let it go.

When we got home from school that afternoon, mum was waiting for us. She had some sad news for us; that nanna had passed away at around 1.30 that afternoon. Just before she passed, she had told my Aunty, I can go now, I have just been to see all my moko (grandchildren) before drifting off into eternal sleep. I like to think that the whirlwind was nana coming to say goodbye to me, so that is a special memory for me.

The next day was spent preparing for the tangi (funeral) which was to be held at the old Nga Hau e Wha, (The Four Winds) which was the local Marae (meeting place) in Pukekohe. These Hui customarily last for a three-day period with the actual funeral being on the third day. To me personally, I find the whole experience as an amazing way to celebrate someone's life and acknowledgement of their being in our midst during their lives and their own individual journey.

By this stage in my life, Maori Culture had begun to be accepted in schools in Pukekohe, even to the extent that the schools that we attended allowed groups representing the school to attend the tangi to pay respects to our nanna, while also experiencing the Marae experience first-hand. I thought that was cool as did friends of ours that were in the group.

All the karakia and services were in the Maori language, which I didn't understand, but the experience itself was quite overwhelming. Our parents were telling us what to do and when we were not required in the main hall, we worked behind the scenes preparing food, cleaning dishes and doing whatever else needed to be done at the time.

The coming together of whanau in such large numbers was new for me and I found I was meeting relatives I never even knew existed. This was the first of many times that I would experience this throughout my life.

It was a good way to talk with cousins and get to know the ones we had never met before and this built a bond between us that is still strong today. Unfortunately, I have found during my lifetime that these occasions only really happen at weddings and funerals. It is a sad reality, and I believe we should all attempt to keep in touch more often and for happy occasions as well as the sad.

The last night before the funeral, it is customary for everyone to settle into the main hall after dinner to celebrate the life of the deceased. The main hall has mattresses all around the wall for people to sleep on, and you found yourself a place to make up a bed. Us young ones were grouped up with a few cousins near our dad, as mum was with her family to watch over her mother until the funeral. At a tangi, the body is never to be left alone and the immediate family take turns keeping company with the body until the time of the funeral.

A walking stick is passed around to every person in the room and when you receive it, you are to stand up, state your name where you are from and how you are related to the deceased, which requires you to know a little bit about your whakapapa (family tree). If you have any stories to share about experiences you shared with the deceased, you are then encouraged to tell them, and to finish off, you then offer a waiata (song) before passing the walking stick to someone else to do the same. The passing of the walking stick is continued until everyone in the room has spoken and usually goes all night till dawn.

Mum had told us what we needed to know so that we could follow the protocols of the Marae. It was an overwhelming experience but all of us young ones took it in our stride.

The korero (talking) was still going on when I woke up in the early hours of the morning. Some of the stories had many laughing at the story being told, but it was all in Maori, so I never understood any of it. I sat up to look around and noticed some movement through the glass doors at the entry to the hall. There were double opaque glass doors, and entry area and then the actual entry doors on the other side of the foyer.

I thought it was just another group of people gathering in the entrance preparing to enter the main hall and paid no attention. It had happened so many times over the past few days.

All the other kids around me were asleep at this time and I have no idea what the time was, I just knew it was late because so many of the people in the hall were also asleep.

I turned to look up at the entrance door again and I could still see movement through the glass doors. I kept watching and waiting for them to come in when suddenly in they came, a group of them. What scared me was that they did not open the doors, they walked straight through them. I could not believe what I was seeing, and my fear levels went through the roof. I dived under the blankets and stayed there too afraid to move and fell asleep. The next thing I knew, I was woken by people packing up the bedding, getting dressed and preparing for the funeral.

I have never told anybody about what I saw, I would have only been told I was being stupid as normal but now I see it at almost every funeral I go to and just accept it. I now know it is our Tupuna (Ancestors) coming to claim one of their own and welcoming them to the other side. Now that I understand how this all works, it gives me a feeling of relief, joy and pride, knowing that the loved ones that we have just said our goodbyes to are in good hands.

Despite all the other beliefs about heaven and hell, I have been shown there is no such thing as hell and hell was only introduced by mankind as a way of controlling the masses. If you believe there is hell, then you will manifest and create a hell in your own mind creating fear and submission.

Do yourself a favour and denounce not only hell but also those who used it to control the masses and walk in peace knowing you have unshackled yourself from the earthly bounds of constraint.

We are here to learn to love and forgive with compassion, empathy and respect. Unfortunately, most of us have only learnt how to work, eat, sleep and accumulate material things.

I too have been guilty of this in the past but would like to think I have identified the problem and have made or am in the process of making further changes to balance my lifestyle out. Just remember that the love we are to learn is to love one another, not love of a car, a bike or anything else materialistic. We need to be love, share love and give love to each other.

For me personally, the most empowering love I have had the privilege of experiencing during one of my astral travels is all-encompassing love. I encountered all-encompassing love in another dimension during an astral travel in which I was given information about some of the objectives regarding the role I have been prepared for.

As a result of my astral travel, I now know that I had been summoned to the other side in order that information could be directly given to me in regard to my responsibilities for the role I have chosen to accept. All-encompassing love is everywhere, it resides in every living being, in every lifeform, in every innate object, in all of the elements of nature it is everywhere. When you experience this, you will be overcome with compassion, your spirit will lift your body to float above the ground and you will even feel it as you inhale. All-encompassing love is everywhere, it just is. I have been privileged to experience it and have known no experience like it. After I had returned to my body, I was so energised I could feel energy all over the surface of my skin all over my body. At one stage while I was doing a lot of astral travelling, I found I would touch kitchen appliances and they would blow up at my touch. Microwaves, toasters and kettles I have done them all. It got to the stage where I had to get Leanne to cook toast, boil the jug and use the microwave or I would just blow them up.

Getting back to the story of my youth, at this point in my life I was only a kid and as I was a kid and could not talk to anybody about what was happening to me, I felt very isolated and alone. This seemed to be the norm, with people I have met with a gift, during my journey so far. It has resulted in all of us experiencing some very dark days in our lifetimes and after sharing these instances with each other we found that the similarities with how we were treated by others and the feeling of isolation, loneliness and recklessness was very similar in all cases. On a positive note, now that we had met and shared our stories, we now know that we are not alone any longer. Funnily enough, our life paths crossed at a time when we most needed to know that we were not alone and then we all moved along on our own journeys in different directions, but we were there for each other when we each needed it.

I personally was at a point in my teenage years where I didn't care if I lived or died. I ran my life to the limit everyday recklessly living my life with abandon. During these years I almost succumbed to doing myself in to relieve myself of all the visions and anger I was experiencing with increasing frequency. I was in a dark place, again feeling very alone and isolated at that stage of my life. Funnily enough, I found quite a few years ago that some members of my family still see me as that same person I was in my teens so I decided that rather than explain to them who I am now and where I have been and what I have become, it is easier for me to put on an act when I visit home and see family and let them see who they think I am. My life journey is mine and I don't believe I need to explain or justify it to members of my family or anyone else for that matter, so I just continue to let them see me through the eyes they saw me in my teens. It is neither here nor there to me.

At times I would talk to myself aloud and ask whether this really was a gift I had received, or a burden. Many times, the line became very blurred. I remember on numerous occasions hiding under my blankets and crying myself to sleep thinking to myself 'Why me'. I was not crying because I was afraid, it was that what I had considered to be a burden back then was becoming bigger and bigger and at times too much of a weight for this young boy to carry.

I became very thick skinned and turned to alcohol and drugs to help me to escape what was tormenting me more and more as time went on. I mean, I was still having visions or dreams that would sometimes scare the shit out of me and have me waking up screaming during the night trying to fight someone who was not there but no one wanted to listen to what I had to say or help me come to terms with what was happening to me, so I just suffered in silence. I managed to hide my pain to those around me by developing a wicked sense of humour, which can be wild at times, along with a cheekiness which seemed to piss quite a few people off. In all honesty it was these two attributes which most helped me to overcome the weight I was carrying. I make no apology for being a cheeky shit or for pissing people off. It helped me at the time and at the time that was all that mattered.

Again, I really need to thank Pa Henare Tate, Leanne Walters, Ron and Leonie Meikle, Aunty Annie Kira and Aunty Katie Raumati. Without you all in my life at that time, I really do not know what would have become of me.

In hindsight it really does look like I was being watched over and some of my angels at the time were earth bound even though I did not know it at the time.

CHAPTER 3

Simmering Away Like A Boil-Up

In the following years I could sense something building inside of me but still not being able to talk to anyone about what was happening I had to find a way to deal with it myself. All I could think to do was to take it within and try to come to terms with it or try to run from it. I went further inside myself in order to try to confront or protect myself. To be honest I am not sure which.

At the time, one thing that even I noticed was that I was developing a real temper and I didn't know why. In later years I realised it was the warrior, my inner heritage, boiling away just below the surface. It had been impatiently waiting to be bought into the light.

During this time mum and dad decided to dismantle nannas house in Pukekohe and rebuild it at Mitimiti. My Uncle Ian and Aunty Maryanne had built a new house on the property so there was no need for it anymore.

We spent months dismantling and moving the timber from the property on Pukekohe Hill to our home in Helvetia Rd. Dad had also asked Mr Barnaby, the pensioner next door, if we could use his back yard to store the materials. By the time we stacked all the timber in his backyard it really did look like a timber yard.

On weekends and after school if we were not working in the market gardens, we all pitched in de-nailing timber so it could be pre-cut into the house we were to rebuild on the farm.

Prior to Xmas of 1976, the bundles of building materials were loaded onto a truck and trailer and we all packed up and headed off to Mitimiti for a holiday but more importantly, to build a house.

There are many builders in our whanau and extended whanau whom all came north to help with the build. I still find it amazing that we pulled up one day and parked this truck and trailer in a paddock and seven days later there was a 3-bedroom house at lock up stage.

The house still stands today and now belongs to my sister Georgina and her whanau as a holiday Bach. It stands on the coast with amazing sea views but in this part of the country, all sea views are amazing.
We spent every holiday up there from then on. It is an amazing place with so much natural beauty and breath-taking scenery.

It was in 1978 that mum and dad decided that mum and the three youngest boys would move back to Mitimiti and live in the Bach while dad would stay in Pukekohe with the rest of the family to work and try to sell the house.

We moved up to the farm in the May school holidays and

Andrew and I were enrolled in Panguru High school while the youngest brother, Malcolm was enrolled at Matihetihe Primary School.

Mum started a job as a forestry worker, and we started our new life here. It was different during the year as there were no holiday makers and the place was deserted and quiet, I really liked it. I made some good friends at Panguru High school and to this day we are still good friends.

The High School was classified as the smallest High School in New Zealand at the time with around 37 students. I found myself being immersed in our culture and got to hear many of the stories from our elders on the Marae, which gave me a great sense of belonging and pride.

I also discovered many of the funnier sides of life with some real characters of the region. There are many instances where the humour of some of the people would have you in stitches and to this day, remembering these moments still brings a smile to my face.

My older brother Andrew was too set in his ways to stay up here and he moved back to Waiuku to live with my older brother John and his wife to finish his schooling which left mum, my younger brother Mal and myself living on the farm. Ironically today Andrew is the only brother living at Mitimiti.

I loved living at Mitimiti and look back at those days with great fondness.

On most Friday afternoons, I would take the bus ride home from school, have something to eat, catch my horse and I would be off. I would not arrive home again till Sunday afternoon. I would spend the weekend with a group of mates, Joe Thomas, Renata Maaka, Stephen Maclean as well as others and we would ride around on horseback everywhere without a care in the world. One time we rode 35 kms to a disco to get there in time for the last song. We met up with some local girls, stayed in town for the night in a barn sleeping in the hay and rode home again the next day.

One day I was on the school bus going home when I saw an elder by the name of Pako, an uncle from our extended whanau. He had bought two buses to use as accommodation and was digging out a bank in order to park his buses where he wanted them. I got home and caught my horse and rode back out to where I saw him which was about a 6 km ride. I just rode in, tied up my horse started talking with him and picked up a shovel to help him dig. I did this for a few days until the area was clear, then on the next day on the bus home I saw that he had the two buses in position. He was grateful for the assistance and unbeknown to me, his family would return the favour to me many years down the track.

Life was good, and you just helped people out......because you could.

The Murray family stayed in our old homestead and they had moved back to their own farm further north in Whangape and another uncle moved into the house for the remainder of the lease of the property. My uncle Puddy, as we called him, was an absolute character, funny as and I would drive him around in his cars to wherever he wanted to go. I was thirteen at the time with no licence and driving on some of the worst roads in New Zealand. I loved it.

He used to tell lots of stories many of them funny as hell, but I knew that if he was telling me something in a serious tone......I needed to listen. Puddy would have a thousand and one funny stories to tell and you never had a dull conversation with him. The house had gained quite a bit of notoriety due to stories of ghosts or kehua being seen at the property by several people at different times. It had also gained a bit of notoriety with some of the stuff my uncle used to do while he lived there, hilarious stuff that I cannot divulge here. At first these stories of ghosts scared the bejeezus out of me. Remember...I had also seen someone when I first ever visited the place.

At first, I was quite apprehensive about the place but as time wore on, I became very comfortable with the place and ended up basically living there with my uncle, or even staying there on my own when he was away on the odd occasion.

At times I would endure some very scary experiences such as seeing balls of light zooming around the room so I would run down the hill to the Bach with my mum and brother. It was after these episodes that I found it harder to comprehend what was happening to me. As I said earlier, I had no one to talk to about it for fear of being scoffed at or told I was being stupid or silly, so I just suffered in silence.

An opening as the school bus driver came available and dad got the position, so he left Pukekohe and moved back up to the farm with us. The following year the lease expired on the farm, so we all moved into the homestead and reconnected with the property.

I still saw many things while we were living there but the fear of the visions was balanced by the amazing energy, I would experience just by being there. I would see things and get messages I did not understand and while fear was taking its grip on me, I still remembered those messages even in the state of fear.

Later in life I would discover that these snippets of information such as the visions or local history and stories from elders at the Marae, would come into play with what I was doing at that time. The thing is, when I was told something or experienced different things that did not really make sense to me for one reason or another, I would acknowledge it and set it to the side as it were. Further along in my journey, I found that when I went looking for something in particular, all of those small snippets of information that I had set aside suddenly popped back into my memory and completed the picture I was looking for in much the same way as a jigsaw puzzle. Sounds bizarre I know but I would see a video like picture in my mind and these snippets would zoom in to the picture to complete it. For me that was just how it works it is difficult to explain really but it was at that point I realised that I had been given small pieces of information in random sequences my entire life that I would be able to recall during my journey. I had discovered another tool I had been given to assist me on my journey and in recent years I have utilised it much more frequently as I needed. It will become clear when I relate it to certain stories further along in my journey.

I have learnt to accept my role and to trust that what is supposed to happen will happen.

Being submersed in my own culture with such an amazing landscape and the history of the area really began to take a hold of me in an awesome way. I took up Maori carving at school and was involved in producing a carved mural depicting the local legend of the Maori Chief Kupe arriving in the Hokianga. We were one of the schools who took part in a 4 -day culture fest with the other schools being from Opononi, Te Kao and Broadwood.

The mural was presented to the Waitangi Marae as part of a school project between our school and three other schools, all of which presented their own murals containing a local legend relevant to their area in order to hang them all in the wharekai on the Marae so as to represent northern Maori history.

Before I left High School, I undertook to produce another mural with the help of some friends who were also involved in the original mural at Waitangi. We presented this mural to our High School and it represented the legend of Panguru Mountain, so it was very relevant to the area and well received by the local elders and teachers who attended the presentation to the school.

At each of these presentations I made speeches in Maori,

memorised of course, but not understanding what I was saying. I wish that I had taken the time to learn my own language but unfortunately, I did not. It was not until much later in life that I discovered that maybe there was a reason I did not learn it. That reason would present itself much further along in my journey when I was taught how spirituality goes beyond how the Maori interpreted it. During my training with the mentoring from my Tupuna, I was told not to learn the language or Te Reo just yet as I still need to work outside of the Maori Culture, without regret or inner conflict, in order to learn how much further my spirituality can take me without being under the collective umbrella of Maoridom. If I were to learn my language now, those lessons and experiences would no longer be available to me. I was told that when I had been shown everything I needed to know, it was only then that I could learn Te Reo and take my place under the Maori cultural umbrella. Certain lessons had to be undertaken before the language was learnt or I could no longer access that knowledge contained in those lessons. From where I stand, I accept what I have been told and I know that some of the things I have already seen, has given me a whole new perspective on our relativity to spirituality in relation to where we fit into the global picture of indigenous races. I can honestly say that I do understand why I must learn what they are teaching me before going under that umbrella as it were, I had no idea we were part of something so big.

It was at times like these that I really discovered myself and my identity as well as a sense of why I am here, in this life living and what it is that I am to achieve.

With the benefit of hindsight, after some time has passed you are able to look back at where you were, where you are standing now, and where you are going in the future. It is then that you begin to understand how and why things are and how they have happened. You will find that you will be surprised by the results. I now know what it means when I hear the phrase, to go forward you must look back. It is empowering to see how far your own journey has bought you.

I left home just after I turned 15 and headed to Waiuku in South Auckland. I stayed with my oldest brother John and his wife at the time Barbara and began looking for work.

I was keen for work and took on anything I could get my hands on. I took on work in orchards, a builder's T/A, and then ended up as a contract fencer erecting farm fencing all over the Waikato. It was a good job and the money was good but eventually I applied for a job with New Zealand Steel, and began work at Glenbrook.

During this time, things were going very well for me and nothing out of the ordinary happened except for the constant feeling of a weight being on my shoulders. I still had no idea what it was or even what it represented, it was just a feeling after all.

I lived hard and worked hard but even I noticed again that my temper was getting worse and worse. I could feel something inside building up again but had no idea what was going on. I felt like I was walking on eggshells.

The visions had started again just before I turned 18 and as always, I kept them to myself for fear of being branded a nutcase I suppose. It wasn't until one day I visited my Aunty Katie, who was a loving kind soul. She asked how things were going and I just opened to her about what was really going on with me. She embraced me and started to cry. For the first time in my life I felt relief that someone understood what I was going through. It was nice to finally have an understanding ear that could empathise with the situation I was facing.

Being a religious person, she offered prayers for me and offered help wherever she could in order to ease the burden for me. She did explain to me the belief that one person from each generation was given the gift of being a seer. A seer being someone who is capable of seeing things and more precisely people, dead people to be blunt. She told me that it is usually the youngest or the oldest of the family and more likely to be a boy.

She told me the so-called gift was the passing down of mana from one generation to another. The translation of mana, being the importance, knowledge, strength, power and spiritual capability. The mana being from the procession of Chiefs who had walked this earth before my time.

At the time I just sat there dumbfounded to what I was hearing. I really could not comprehend what I was hearing or understand the full ramifications of what I was being told, so I just sat in silence trying to make heads or tails of it. I could not do either.

I stayed for dinner, which as always was a lovely spread when you visited Aunty Katie. Before I left, she asked me if I had told my mother to which I replied, "yes I have". I told her but she just mocked me and told me I was being stupid and that was why I had never told anyone else about what was going on until now. She sighed and said, I do not know why that sister of mine will not tell you about this stuff, you need to know it and she knows about it. She then asked me how I felt about it and I told her I did not want anything to do with it. To me at the time it was not a gift it was more of a burden, affecting me in so many ways it was not funny and to top it off I knew that it was responsible for my out of control behaviour and temper. There was no way I wanted any part of it.

She did give me a warning before I left. She told me to be very careful, it is a very powerful force we were dealing with. I gave her a hug and left and although I never had all the answers, I felt a bit more relaxed, if that is the right word. I finally found someone I could talk to.

I remember that night reciting the Lord's Prayer and asking that they choose someone else and to just leave me alone. I wanted my life back. Subsequently, as is evident by me writing this book, no such luck.

Not long after this, a spiritual event took place back at Mitimiti which really created a lot of excitement not only in our community but also in Waiuku where I was living.

A woman by the name of Dulcie, an aboriginal clairvoyant, had a vision where an old Maori woman told her to travel to the South Island to collect four Taonga. These Taonga were to be returned to the four spiritual corners of the Maori world in order to restore peace in the Maori spiritual world. The first of the four corners are in the South Island, so a Taonga was presented to a Marae in the South Island. The second was Tahuna Pa in Waiuku, so she returned that Taonga to Tahuna Pa. Through visions, she sketched where the next item was to be returned to by way of a drawing. The drawing was of the Mitimiti Marae, which was eventually recognised, and the wheels were set in motion to initiate that Taonga return.

The local people of Tahuna Pa, the Marae in Waiuku, hired a bus to return the patu to Mitimiti along with a local contingent to accompany it on its trip home. A video camera was positioned on the Taonga during the voyage during which its appearance changed from a grey stone colour when it left Waiuku, to greenstone with ingrained blood stains by the time it arrived at the Mitimiti Marae. Obviously a very powerful force was at work here, one which I did not understand at the time. To be honest when I heard what happened I got a chill down my spine.

The discovery generated much interest around the country and was reported on the news and in newspapers. I always wondered how these things happened and why. It was not until I was much older that I discovered the answer. I did not travel home for the Hui where it was presented back to our Marae, but it is housed in Hato Hemi church to this day. A few months later, a contingent from our Marae visited Tahuna Pa in Waiuku to thank them for returning the Taonga to its rightful home. Mum and dad were part of the contingent as dad was one of our Marae elders, so I went out after work one night to see everyone and sit in on proceedings for a couple of hours.

There was a buzz of excitement there and I heard a bit more about what had happened and how it now meant a bond had been created between the two Marae as well as the two peoples. Although the message from the clairvoyant was that these items needed to be returned in order to restore peace in the Maori spiritual world there was much debate about just what this message meant.

The next morning the Mitimiti contingent once again boarded the bus and headed further south to Taranaki with a contingent from Tahuna Pa and Dulcie in order to return the fourth item to its final home in Taranaki.

My mother told me that at first the Taranaki people would not accept the Taonga and tried to say it did not belong to them. During the Hui they recognised that it was for them and accepted it back to its home.

I always wondered how it could be that an innate object could be possessed with such power as to call to be taken home.

Things went along as normal for the next year or so but the weight I felt on my shoulders never relented. I found that by partying hard I could get a bit of relief from that constant feeling as it could become very intense at times.

I partied hard and ran amok doing some crazy stuff that really should have gotten me locked up, but it just never happened. I was reckless in everything I did and used laughter to hide what was really going on inside. I had become so used to going within it almost happened automatically every time I had an experience. I found that partying hard gave me a release and relief from the world I was in even if it was only for a few hours.

It was around this time that I met a girl, Leanne, who worked for my then sister in law Barbara as an apprentice hairdresser and we started dating. She was the daughter of a farmer and would eventually become my wife. I enjoyed her company and she seemed to create a bit of balance within me, so I did not need to rely on partying hard so much anymore. She was fun to be around, and it was such a breath of fresh air considering what I had been going through for many years. To be honest, with the benefit of hindsight, I feel sorry that she was exposed to so much of the turmoil and anger that was boiling within me. But there is a reason that people come into our lives and it would be a long way down the road until I would be able to look back and see why she had come into mine. Now that I know why she entered my life all I can say is a very sincere thank you Leanne. Without your actions I would not know what I know now, and I would never have begun or experienced this amazing journey. In fact, I can honestly say that if I had not meet you when I did, I doubt I would be here now to tell the tale and I believe you would agree with me on that, so again, a heartfelt thank you.

I was living in Waiuku at the time in a single men's house in an area known as the block and Leanne was still living at home with her parents. I would go out and stay for dinner quite often with Leanne and her parents Ron and Leonie. Leonie was an amazing cook and I loved going there for dinner. After the first visit bread became a staple on the dinner table. At times I would have them all over to my house for dinner and we would also go out quite a bit. I believe that Leanne's mum Leonie was in tune with quite a few things, as at times when we would speak, she would tell me stuff like she was reading my thoughts. I remember one time I was doing a drawing of a tree on a hill blowing in the wind. I used drawing as a way of releasing. To me, that is what it was. To her she described the turmoil and darkness I had experienced during my lifetime so far. Although I had not told her any of this, she was scarily spot on with what she was saying. It really freaked me out and I tried to pass it all off as being insignificant but inside I was spinning out. How could she know that about me? The conversation stopped and the subject was never raised again. I think she sensed my irritability and respected me enough to not bring it up and make me uncomfortable again, which I thank her for.

She really became a tower of strength for me in many ways as she was very easy to talk to and we really got on well. I must admit, that in times when I was dealing with things spiritual Leonie was right there with Leanne offering support. For this I will always be grateful to them both.

Leanne also had a brother Paul and Lori, his girlfriend at that stage (now married), who lived about ten mins down the road from the farm.

One night they invited us all around for dinner so Leanne and I and her parents headed down for dinner. Dinner was running a bit late, so we were having a few beers. Paul started telling me of an adze (Maori axe head) he had found while he was tramping around the Manukau Peninsula. He was right into tramping back then and would do it most weekends. We went out to the garage and he pulled it out for me to have a look at. It was still sharp and could easily have split a head or two if it were to be put to the test.

It was quite a nice piece and displayed definite signs of age. I held it and did not feel anything out of the ordinary other than how cold it was to touch and how my hand felt cold even after I had put it down. We went back inside and had dinner and then sat around relaxing and just talking. Lori pulled out some photos to show Leanne and her mum Leonie who passed them along for Ron (Leanne's dad) and me to have a look at. I started feeling uneasy and then I was spun right out.

As I was looking at the first photo, the clouds in the photo began to move and change shape. I changed photos but it was the same, every photo I looked at the clouds would change shape in forms and sometimes faces that I did not recognise. I pulled Leanne to the side and said to her do you see anything funny? She looked at the photos then giving me a puzzled look answered no, one after the other she would say no. Only problem was, as she was saying no, I was seeing them move. This went on for about fifteen mins and then I got a droning noise like high voltage power in a substation that started ringing in my head. The noise slowly got louder and louder.

I pulled Leanne aside and said, I have got to get out of here. I told her again about the clouds moving and the ringing in my head getting louder and louder. We made an excuse so as not to cause alarm and left.

The further we got away from the house the quieter the ringing in my head became and by the time we got back to the farm it had gone all together. We parked the car, then as Leanne opened the car door, I could hear that noise again, like it was travelling along the power lines running up the valley. I told Leanne to close the door and lock it. The noise then surrounded the car and began ringing in my head louder than before. Leanne could not hear the noise, but it was driving me mad. We stayed there in the car until Leanne's parents got home before we moved into the house. I sat in front of a gas heater with all four bars running but stayed as cold as ice and shivering. I felt ashamed about freaking out in front of Leanne's parents but was surprised when they were very supportive. I explained the visions and experiences I have had in the past and asked Leanne to call my brother Harry and Aunty Katie. I needed support and I needed it now. Leanne also called her brother Paul who came up to the house. I explained to everyone what I had seen and the noise that was still rattling my brain constantly.

Leanne told Paul that she had called Harry and Aunty Katie and they were on their way. They decided to go and move my car so that the people coming could drive straight up to the back deck and into the house as the wind had also picked up.

They came back inside after about fifteen mins and told me they could not move the car. They could start it, but the park brake refused to come off. It just would not come off at all. The car was left where it was, and we waited for the arrival of my brother and Aunty.

Aunty Katie had some experience with this type of thing and bought Uncle Jimmy and her priest with her. My brother Harry and his then wife Janice also came out. I was still shivering in front of the heater when they arrived and remembered how cold the adze had made my hand earlier in the evening.

I explained to them what had happened and Aunty Katie initialised karakia along with the priest. I can honestly say that the karakia did help, I began to thaw out and the noise in my head slowly subsided until it was gone just before dawn. During the karakia I saw a vision in my mind. I was running down a dark tunnel and could see a light at the end of the tunnel. I kept running and running as the light got bigger and brighter. As I approached the end of the tunnel, I saw the old homestead at Mitimiti. I knew then that I had to go home.

Old Mitimiti Homestead with Post Office to the left

I told Leanne what I had seen and that I had to get home as fast as I can. Aunty Katie told us that if I had to go home wait until daylight. I managed to get a couple of hours sleep as dawn was breaking, then woke up to find everyone was still there. I said again, I need to go home. I went outside and got into my car. It worked perfectly again, and I drove it straight out onto the front lawn with no problems. Everyone was amazed as it would not move during the night.

Leanne's mum told us she would feel better if we took her car after what happened with my car the previous night, so we quickly threw some clothes in a bag then before we left the priest again offered karakia to bless our journey and the vehicle.

I rang mum and dad and told them we would be up to the farm that day, to which they replied we might not get there as a stretch of the road called the skyline had been washed out by heavy rain and had not been reopened. They told us to go the long way around through Broadwood.

We hit the road and I was still feeling uncomfortable and unsure as we headed north. I could still see the vision in my mind of the homestead, telling me to go home.

The old Kendall Homestead Mitimiti, Northland, New Zealand

The further we got north into Ngapuhi country the more relaxed I became and the more at ease I got. Leanne said my driving got less erratic as we got further north.

We got up to Ohaewai which is the last chance turnoff to get the car ferry across Hokianga Harbour and as I could still see the homestead in my mind, I decided to go via Rawene and the ferry hoping the skyline had been reopened by the time we got there.

We drove down to Rawene and boarded for the crossing on the car ferry. When we drove off the ferry, I prayed the road was open and we turned left to head for the coast. Just as fate would have it, the skyline was just being opened to traffic as we arrived, so we went straight through and carried on out to the farm. The roads were a mess with the Northland clay wet and slippery over the last 30 kms but somehow, we just went straight through. I felt a huge relief when we got back to the farm. We sat down with mum and dad and told them what had happened.

I told mum I needed help with this and decided to call our local priest, Pa Henare Tate. Father Tate has known our family for many years in Pukekohe when we were growing up and then at Mitimiti when we moved home. He is not only a Catholic priest but also a local Maori from Motuti with much knowledge of our history, heritage, language, and customs.

I called him and explained what had happened to which he replied to go straight in to see him. Leanne and I drove straight into Panguru to see him. He met us at the front door examining all around me as I entered. We quickly exchanged greetings and I then proceeded to explain to him what was happening about the adze Leanne's brother had found. While I was talking, I still noticed him looking all around me. He questioned me about everything I had done recently and what areas of the country I had been in trying to ascertain what the actual cause of all of this was.

He told me that the 'thing' was still with me, he could see it attached to the top of my face and then proceeded to tell me what it was.

He asked me if I had experienced anything out of the usual recently to which I replied with the events that happened at Paul and Lori's with the photos and the adze Paul had discovered on one of his treks.

He explained that the recent returning home of a Taonga by the people of Tahuna Pa in Waiuku, to our Marae in Mitimiti, has now created a connection between their tribe and ours. As a result, he believed the adze found by Leanne's Brother Paul, was a Taonga of Tahuna Pa and was calling to be returned home.

That calling had been directed through me due to the recent connection between the two tribes and my coming into possession of it.

I told him about the car episode on the night of the happenings to which he replied, if I had left immediately, as I wanted to in my car, I probably would not have made it as the hours of darkness are the hours of the spiritual world. He praised my Aunty Katie for having a priest bless our journey and vehicle but said there was still much to do.

He advised me that I needed to return to Waiuku straight away, collect the Taonga from Paul, Leanne's brother, and return it to the elders of Tahuna Pa immediately. He told me that they will not want to accept it as there is a possibility that someone may die as a result of accepting it, but he said to me very sternly, do not leave until they take it.

Once again, he blessed our journey and vehicle and we headed back to the farm to say goodbye to mum and dad, have a quick bite and then go on our way back to Waiuku.

We managed to catch the last 5 pm ferry back to Rawene and heard later on the radio that just after we had crossed over the skyline it was again closed to traffic due to the conditions. I remember saying to Leanne, we were meant to make the journey. The roads only opened long enough to get us in and out and, as it turned out, the skyline was closed for another month after we passed through due to the conditions and roadwork's required to get it back up to standard.

Anyway, we got back to Leanne's parents at Pollock around 11 pm. Paul had already dropped the adze off there as we had called him before we left Mitimiti. We called Aunty Katie and told her what we had been told to do. She offered to come out to do a karakia for us, but I declined that and said I would do one myself as I just needed to get this done.

We put the adze in the car and said karakia before we headed off back into Waiuku to hand it over to the local elders.

We never gave any notice we were coming, we just turned up on the doorstep of one of the elders. As we pulled into the driveway, the news on the car radio came on. It was midnight on the dot.

Leanne and I went to the door, there were no lights on, and I knocked on the door. I kept knocking until I got a response from someone on the inside. At first, they would not open the door, choosing to talk through it rather than open it. Really, when I think about it if it were me, I would have done the same.

I explained I was from Mitimiti and they had recently returned one of our Taonga and then the door opened. It was a middle-aged woman that opened the door and I proceeded to explain to her what had happened over the last 26 hours.

She listened and at first refused to take the adze and then I told her I would not be leaving until she, or someone from Tahuna Pa, took it off my hands. I remained respectful but firm in what I was saying, and she was very apprehensive about the whole situation. She spoke of Maori belief on the returning of these objects to which I replied I had already been told of this.

After about 40 mins, which seemed like hours, she finally said I could leave it, but she would not handle it personally. She asked me to place it on the floor.

She opened the door further to allow me in and I only went in far enough to place the adze on the floor to the side of the doorway and then retreated out onto the front porch.

Leanne and I thanked her. She did not reply, she just stared at the adze and then at me.

We went back to the car and headed back to Leanne's parents farm where Leonie was still waiting up for us. We had a cup of tea and told her how it all went and then got in to bed exhausted. We never woke up the next day until about 10am. We got up, showered, and then went in for breakfast which Leonie had prepared for us.

As we sat down for breakfast, Leonie told us that Aunty Katie had called that morning. The grandmother of the family we had dropped the adze off to had passed away that morning at 6 am. I did not know really what to make of it. We had been told that someone may die when we returned the adze and now that it had happened, I really did not know how I felt. All I could do was offer a prayer in silence and hope that this lady's passing was just a natural occurrence and not as a result of us returning that adze. I had heard many stories over the years of Taonga or objects calling to go home. I had always wondered how this came to be and it was during my training later in life that the answer was shown to me.

In pre-European times, Maori of old were far more spiritual in their daily life than we are today. The weapons of the warrior and other Taonga were treated as extensions of one's body. Ultimately there were a couple of reasons for this at that time. One was to increase mana another was to ensure good hunting and finally it was to ensure victory in battle. This was done by placing one's own spiritual energy into these innate objects. This is done in much the same way we do today in modern meditational techniques such as putting your energy into a crystal, candle or even a meditation space. The only difference is that today we put energies into tools to assist us in peaceful ways rather than in weaponry. Well at least I do. I believe that even after the owner has passed over, their energy is still contained in these objects and as a result these objects call to be returned home as the energy contained within carries the same individual emotional and cultural ties as the original host. I know it sounds amazing but that is what I was shown, and I have no reason to doubt my Tupuna. When I think more about it, I find it makes absolute sense. Should you find yourself coming into possession of any old Maori artefacts (Taonga) be sure to treat these objects with the utmost respect that they deserve. They come from a different time where spirituality as well as the karakia and incantations that were commonly used, was very powerful and were administered by someone of great mana.

Not long after this Leanne and I began living together, sharing a unit with another couple we knew. This time was marked with several incidents including what I saw as a spiritual test by a member of my own family. I saw her face during the vision and rang her and confronted her about it. I was angry as I had asked in the past for help and she had told me I was being silly, yet she had the audacity to use her energy to put me to test. I was absolutely fuming. It was at this stage I began talking to Leanne about leaving New Zealand to get away from this stuff. We talked about it regularly and struggled to put money away to go.

The decision to consider even leaving New Zealand was causing conflict with family members on both sides and to be honest, the only reason we left so quickly after making our decision was the fact that I had a car accident resulting in my car being written off without me even getting a scratch. The insurance paid out on the car and I just said to Leanne, here is the money, go book two one-way tickets to Australia. We are out of here. Everything happens for a reason eh.

CHAPTER 4

Time to Fly

Leanne and I flew out of New Zealand on June 5th, 1986, with Continental Airlines heading for Melbourne, Australia. Even this was a struggle as we were stranded on the runway in Auckland for 2 hours before finally setting off. As we finally took off from Auckland, I noticed a strange sensation of a weight being lifted off my shoulders. I would discover later that this sensation would happen every time I arrived and left New Zealand.

We landed in Melbourne and were met by my sister Cindy and her husband Jack (we know him as Jack but his birthname is Livio) who, being a real Aussie Italian, picked us up with a carton of beer in the car. We cracked a couple and started heading off for the town they stayed in 2 hours south of Melbourne. I had to crack up. It was my first time in Melbourne, we got lost and I had to tell him how to get out of the city, with the aid of a street map of course. We all thought it was hilarious.

The first few days in Wonthaggi we just relaxed, and I felt a lot lighter for want of a better phrase. We set about looking for work and changing over licences etc. On the weekend we had a bit of a drink and I ended up pulling out the duty-free Johnny Walker whisky.

We were all having a fat old time and it was the early hours of thc morning when I went to our room to grab the last bottle of spirits. I was headed back to the kitchen when I had the overwhelming urge to relieve myself, so I headed off to the toilet tucking the bottle into my jacket. While in the toilet and doing the bizzo, the whisky bottle slipped out of my jacket and into the toilet smashing the bottle and breaking off a big piece of the ceramic toilet bowl at the same time.

Jack rushed into the laundry when he heard the crash, it was loud. I still remember the look of horror when he looked down into the bowl with pieces of ceramic all over the place from the toilet. His hands went all animated and he screamed *'How the hell are we supposed to drink it now'*. I just cracked up laughing as he wasn't worried about the toilet, just the whisky. He has never let me live it down ever since and I still laugh when he reminds me of it.

We spent a lot of time with Mathew and Jenna my niece and nephew and I got to know the movie 'Never Ending Story' almost word for word as Mathew would have it on in an almost endless roll, over and over. The funny thing is that a lot further down the track when I was undertaking spiritual training this was one of the movies that would play in my mind to show me what it was that I was facing at that moment. There were many movies that served that purpose for me and they all came together in my mind like a TV screen, so I knew what it was that I was being shown. I know it sounds a bit funny but that is how it works for me. This would be a good point for you to remember for your journey, firstly, understand how you are to receive information and then be sure to put your trust into it.

Leanne and I both got jobs the following week in a town called Leongatha. She began work in a hairdressing salon and I worked in a Butter Factory.

We bought an old Valiant car. It was old but in good nick as an older guy had restored it prior to us buying it. She was a good runner and reliable as. We would travel to and from work together and when Leanne had her late night on a Thursday I would go to the pub after work and wait for her.

My brother in law Jack worked as a test driver at that stage for GMH, a major car manufacturer, just out of Melbourne at a place called Lang Lang. One day I didn't wait at the pub but went home after work as Jack had already told me he would be bringing a test car home for road trials. We had already planned that we would go pick Leanne up to give it a road test. Leanne knew nothing of these arrangements.

I got home and waited for Jack to get home and talked my sister into coming for a ride as well and we could get a pub meal for dinner. So off we went and just out of town I swapped with Jack so I could have a drive of it.

The trip usually took 30 to 35 minutes in the Valiant and I did it in twenty mins in this test car. It drove like a dream. We pulled up outside of where Leanne worked, and I pulled up and double-parked outside of the shop and tooted the horn. She was looking all around, and I got Jack to wind down the passenger window so I could get her attention. She jumped in the back seat all excited and asked whose car it was. I told her it was ours, that I had traded in the Valiant and got $800 dollars for it and it was only another $23,990 and this baby was all ours. Man did she spit it. She went all quiet. I said, I am so excited let's go to the pub for dinner, my shout.

Standing in the pub at the counter I said to Leanne, what are you having for dinner, she stared at the floor and said, the kid's meal, that is all we can afford now. I cannot believe you would make a big decision with this without talking to me first. Then she went to the toilet. My sister followed her and told her I was pulling her leg and it was a test car. She came back to me and tore a strip off me while I was just laughing my head off. I loved pulling pranks on her.

I had noticed the spiritual things that were affecting me back home seemed to leave me alone here, so I just enjoyed being allowed to be me. The only thing I did not like was the weather. It was cold and wet or both and every night I got home from work I would watch the news and weather and the weather girl would always say how sunny and warm it was in Perth, Western Australia.

I spoke with Leanne and told her I wanted to follow the sun and move on to Western Australia, but she told me she was homesick and wanted to go home. We discussed it for a few days, and I convinced her to head west.

I sold the car and we booked our tickets to leave on the Saturday night from Melbourne on a bus. We decided to go by bus as we had never seen Australia and could not get over the size of the place so we thought we would watch it pass by through a bus window. I didn't know how to tell my sister we were leaving so, like a chicken, I left it till the Friday night then said to her, hey sis, we should go to Melbourne tomorrow night. She said to me, what's up in Melbourne, where do you want to go? To catch our bus I said, we are off. She got a bit upset and tangi tangi (crying) but I knew this was going to happen, that is why I left it so long to tell her.

We headed off to Melbourne the next afternoon, had a meal together and then headed to the depot to board our Greyhound Bus.

We waved to them and our bus headed off into the darkness to start our 3-day journey.

If you ever consider travelling across Australia, do not go by bus. We didn't know it then, but we do now. Sounds romantic, well it did to us, but yeah nah it's not.

In all honesty, it was not that bad. We had a few highlights during the hours of daylight, like coming down off the hills into Adelaide. Beautiful view of the city, the red seal coming over the Nullarbor Plain and there were some characters on the bus which helped relieve the boredom a bit.

Leanne had been in contact with her sister in law who had an uncle in a place called Kambalda, so we decided we would stop off there and check out the work scene as it was a mining town about

65kms south of Kalgoorlie.

After 3 days we pulled into Kambalda at 8am. I got off the bus and it was 42 degrees. I looked at the bus driver and said "Wow...... there is a hell and you just dropped us off here". He just laughed and said you better get used to it if you are going to stay here mate.

We stayed with Mike Sampson and his lovely wife Sheryl and their family for a week or so, found work then moved in with Mike's nephew Hama and his girlfriend Michelle.

The whole town was owned by one mining company but eventually we managed to get a private rental property and then when the mining company sold its houses, we bought one and moved into it.

It was while we were in a property owned by the local butcher Bob Wray in 1987 that we got a phone call from home. The homestead at Mitimiti had burned down due to an electrical fault. Everyone had gotten out ok, but they only had time to grab the TV and everything else went up in flames. I felt a great pain of sadness when I heard this as the old place had always been the place I ran to when I was lost. I felt hopeless not being able to go home, help or even call as mobile phones were not a big thing at this time and there was only the house line which went up in flames.

It seemed to be the end of another chapter in my life. Little did I know that this was not the case at all. One thing that remains the same is the homestead. I always see it in my visions and my astral travels. The kehua, or ghosts and spirits that were attached to the place, have now all passed over. The house fire had cleansed the site and now it is the presence of peace and healing that is experienced when I go home. There had been many instances of people seeing ghosts or kehua at the homestead over the years, myself included. With cleansing I would hope that the healing felt there today will only increase and amplify the energy that is felt there for the benefit of all living things. The reason I say this will be explained much further down the track. The old people had a reason that they built on that site. I discovered that reason much later in life with the help of my Tupuna, information and observations I made as a young man while living there and the result of a field trip I conducted with one of my spiritual students from Perth whom I took back to Mitimiti but that story will be told much later.

Leanne and I were both working in the mining industry at this stage and life was going along as well as can be expected. It was during a visit from her mum Leonie later in 1987 that we decided we were going to get married. In 1988 we returned to New Zealand to get married. Leanne went home a month before I did and although I had no problems while in Australia as soon as I had landed back in Auckland, I felt that familiar weight back on my shoulders. I still did not know what it was but fortunately nothing notable happened during this visit.

We came back to Australia and I must admit, the feeling of that weight leaving my shoulders was very welcome as we departed

Auckland.

We were back in Australia shaping out a life, when in 1990 Leanne fell pregnant.

Up until this time we were quite happy living in Australia but as Leanne was pregnant, we both wanted to go home for the birth so that we could both have family around to share the experience. We did think long and hard about our decision as I knew as soon as I got back to Auckland, I would again be greeted by that weight being placed squarely on my shoulders once more. Even that was not enough to deter us from making the decision to move home.

We put the house up for sale and sold it walk in walk out.

The house sold quickly and all we had to do was pack our clothes and leave. Leanne was approaching 3 months pregnant when we boarded the flight home to New Zealand. On arrival at Auckland Airport, as expected I was once again greeted by that familiar weight resting again squarely on my shoulders. I was home.

CHAPTER 5

Back Home to New Zealand – The First Step

Leanne was happy to be moving home and to see her parents and so was I. We moved in with them on the farm while I looked for work.

For starters, work was hard to come by and I managed to pick up a week at a time here and there doing whatever I could to bring home a paycheck. We did have the sale proceeds of our house in the bank so that helped us out. I also helped around the farm with Ron milking, fencing, and doing some repairs to the milking shed and tractor implements to make things a bit easier for Leanne's dad.

Leanne was enjoying being home with her mother as the pregnancy ran its term and it was good to see the bond between her and her mother bloom.

It was during this time that Loretta, a friend of Leonie's, stopped in one afternoon for a chat and was talking with Leonie about a clairvoyant she had been to see and how accurate her reading was. Loretta and her partner Wally were a lovely couple and Wally would do handyman and renovation work around the area. I was sitting there listening to the conversation about this clairvoyant and I could feel my guard going up.

At this stage, all things spiritual still freaked me out so I was not very open to it. Leanne on the other hand was taking a great interest in what Loretta had to say and was getting right into the conversation. I just sat there listening not really getting involved in the conversation and then I sat up with surprise when Leanne asked for his number saying she would like to see him. This kind of took me by surprise considering all that had happened in the past and I saw this clairvoyant and our past problems as all being cut from the same cloth. All I could think of was trouble, with a capital T.

Leanne rang up and made an appointment for the Saturday morning as I would not be working and could drive her there. For the next three days I tried my best to talk her out of it saying things like 'you told him your name and know he will just do an internet search and find out everything about you'. In truth, the internet was nothing like it is today, it was still relatively new and never had half of the information you can find on there now. As the week went on, my attempts to get her to cancel continued. I was getting quite anxious as I had been told in the past to stay away from this stuff and here was my wife getting involved with it. Well that is how I saw it anyway.

On the Friday I was talking to Leanne again and she was just ignoring what I had to say. Suddenly, I even shocked myself, when out of nowhere I said to her 'Well if he is so good, call him and cancel your appointment and tell him your husband will take the reading instead and do not tell him my name'. Leanne looked at me in shock and just said 'ok then'. I stood there as she rang and changed the appointment to her husband for the Saturday without mentioning my name and then hung up the phone.

Almost immediately I had thoughts going through my head saying, 'you dumbass what did you go and do that for'. I was even contemplating just cancelling the appointment altogether but then thought I would look like a bit of a hypocritical dipstick if I did that. Then I thought to myself, well I will go and prove to them all this is just a load of rubbish.

That evening and during the night, all I could think of were the spiritual episodes I had already endured and the warnings I had been given telling me to have nothing to do with this stuff. The fear inside me began to take a grip on me. I was about to go against everything I had ever been taught about this stuff.

The following morning Leanne was going to come with me, but I put her off telling her to stay home and have a rest and that I would be fine. The truth is, I didn't know what was going to happen, I just did not want her there in case things went bad. That was my rationale at the time, so I just went with it.

On Saturday morning I got up and had breakfast with Leanne, Ron, and Leonie. We had a bit of a chat over breakfast and I think Leanne and her mum could sense the conflict raging inside me regarding ignoring what I had been taught and told as a child. They offered kind words and told me things would be ok. I was very apprehensive about the decision I had taken but decided to get a move on and get it over with. I gave Leanne's belly a huge hug and kiss then got into the car and headed off. The drive was about 40 minutes and during this time these warnings kept flashing through my mind. Those damn logical voices in my head.

I got there fifteen mins early and just sat outside his house chain smoking trying to work up the courage to go in. I must have smoked almost a packet of cigarettes. I looked at my watch, 10am, it's now or never. I got out of the car and walked up to the front door. I was trembling all over.

The door opened and a shortish, one armed guy with longish wispy hair held out his hand and shook mine saying, 'Hi Ron, what are you doing back here in New Zealand. Why didn't you stay in Australia where everything was going so good for you'?

I was blown away with what he said. How could he know. I know Leanne did not give him my name. I was there when she made the call and how did he know we had just moved home to New Zealand, Leanne had not told him anything.

He ushered me into the house and into a room with his reading table. He introduced himself as Graham and told me that the colours around me were amazing and that I had a very strong chiefly presence around me, watching over me.

He then asked me why we came back to New Zealand and I told him we had wanted our first born to be born at home. He said to me, it was not your choice. This boy wanted to be born in New Zealand. It is his birthright and he wanted to claim his birthright. He went on to tell me how well we went in Australia. He then told me that I will get a good job in New Zealand but for the long-term we will end up back in Australia. It is where you need to be for several reasons he said. You need to be in Australia to learn. The learning you need to undergo will not happen if you stay in New Zealand. There are too many obstacles in your path here, too many reasons for you not to learn what you need to learn. I asked him what I needed to learn, and he just told me that I would find out when the time was right, but I had taken the first step by coming to see him today. He went on to tell me some other insights which came into play later along my journey which helped immensely in addressing some side issues that needed to be addressed.

His open manner put me at ease and all the anxiousness I experienced before entering his home soon diminished.

We finished the reading and he gave me his personal number telling me that if I needed guidance at any time feel free to call him. I did call him a couple of times over the next few years. The last time I did contact him we had moved back to Australia as he had told us we would.

A few weeks later I was employed full time with a transport company in the Auckland area. Due to the distance to get to work we decided to move closer to my work.

We ended up renting a house at Clarks Beach on the southern side of Manukau Harbour after mentioning to close friends Todd and Denise Nicole that we needed to move closer to Mangere for work but did not want to be in suburbia. The house was owned by

Denise's parents who used it as a holiday house but agreed to rent it to us for which we were very appreciative.

It was a nice place overlooking the Manukau Harbour and we loved living there.

The views over the harbour were so relaxing and being able to walk along the beach after work was awesome.

Our son Brett was born at Middlemore Hospital in Papatoetoe and then transferred with his mother to Pukekohe Hospital as there were no complications. This was the hospital where both Leanne and I were born.

Once they were released, we went back home to Clarks Beach.

It was only a matter of months when my job description changed to doing Line Haul swap work between Auckland and Wellington overnight for an Auckland Company contracting to a major freight forwarder.

Due to the job being in Mangere we decided to buy a house in Manurewa, again it was to be closer to my work. Well the house was nice and turns out one of the neighbours were the neighbours from hell. We did have a couple of altercations with them but all in all it was not too bad I suppose. The house had high timber fences around, and the backyard was enclosed so we would let Brett crawl around on the grass and Ziggy the cocker Spaniel we bought back from Australia would follow him around keeping an eye on him.

Ziggy, or mort as we called him (short for Ziggymortis family joke) would pander around Brett like an old woman but if anyone came near the fences he would go into protective mode and bark and growl to protect Brett. He was a great dog.

It was from a very early age that things began happening with our son, Brett. It was when he was a year old his mother noticed him having talks with his 'friend'. He used to have frequent talks with his friend and would get upset when his mother said that she could not see him. He did mention the man with the scribbly face, but we thought he was referring to his favourite kid's show, Mr Squiggle, an Aussie children's show that was showing on TV in New Zealand at the time. We thought no more of it.

His grandmother used to take him shopping when they were visiting and even she noticed that she would be at the supermarket thinking about what she was going to get and no sooner had she thought about it, Brett had grabbed it from the shelf and put it in the trolley. This happened on quite a few occasions and every time gran would tell us what had happened.

To be honest, even I noticed it as well on the weekends when I would do servicing or repairs on the two cars or be tinkering on something in the shed. I remember working under the cars on numerous occasions and needed to get another tool. As I went to slide out from under the car, Brett would pass the tool I needed under the car to me. It blew me away to start with and I ran inside to tell his mother all excited.

All of this started happening more regularly and we just accepted it not thinking anything of it.

In fact, in order to spend more time with Brett and let his mum get a better sleep, I started pulling up to the house with a fully loaded B double to pick Brett up in the early hours of the morning when I would get back to Auckland. It was normally about 4am and would still be dark. His mother would pack him a bag before she went to bed. I would pick him up with his bag then carry on and deliver my trailers to the Penrose depot or do any urgent overnight deliveries that had to be done. I would then head back to our yard and drop off the Prime Mover for the dayshift driver before heading home to sleep during the day. When I was working, Leanne used to have Brett sleep with her, it was just easier. She noticed that when I would come to pick Brett up, he would wake up and sit bolt upright in bed waiting for me. Without fail, within half an hour I would pull into the street and Brett would sit there saying dad, dad. This went on for the whole time I picked him up.

It was when he was around 18 months old that Leanne had to work through Christmas with her job, so we decided we would have Christmas together as a family and then Brett and I would head up to Mitimiti for a weeklong holiday.

CHAPTER 6

Brett's Friend

Brett and I headed off to Mitimiti on Boxing Day and got to the farm around 2pm. It was a beautiful sunny day and I got a surprise. As we walked into the house Brett ran straight in to see nanna and pop, he was all excited. He then turned around to face a portrait of Atama Paparangi and yelled out to me, 'hey dad, that's the man with the scribbly face, my friend that comes to see me'.

It started out as a Datsun 120Y station wagon....

then it became a beach basher

He was not frightened or upset, he just told me that and then went on talking with nanna and pop. We all just kind of looked at each other and never said a word. I was surprised both mum and dad never made comment but then again, I was not going to push the situation as I knew they would not talk about this stuff with me. I rang Leanne to tell her what had happened and for the first time since we had been back in New Zealand, I was worried. I never told my parents what was going through my mind, choosing to just put it at the back of my mind until I got back to Auckland so Leanne and I could talk.

Brett and I enjoyed the rest of our holiday, cutting down an old car for a beach buggy and strapping Brett into the passenger's seat with rope then off hooning down the beach. We had an absolute ball cutting sick doing broggies. A tourist bus was down at the beach entrance at one stage full of Asians. They were walking around exploring the rocks on the beach when we came onto the beach with our buggy hooning along the beach. I had to laugh because when they saw us, they started laughing and pointing. We only went down to Taikarawa Creek then turned around and headed back to the house and when we came back past the tourists, they had their cameras out taking pics as we flew past. Brett would get worn out by his old man and had to have a good afternoon nap to keep up. Once everyone was up at the farm just before new year's, all the nieces and nephews also had fun on the rescue ranger hooning around the beach and even the older ones got driving lessons. I was surprised we did not have any problems while on holiday considering who

Brett told us his friend was when pointing to a painting of Atama. I had been expecting the worst but was happy when nothing had eventuated during our stay.

At the end of our holiday we headed back to Auckland and the night I got home, Leanne and I had a good talk about what had happened. I decided to talk to Aunty Katie but upon calling the house I found out that she was away, so Leanne called Aunty Annie in Pukekohe and asked if I could go to see her. We went the next day as it was a Sunday and the last day off that I had before going back to work.

We arrived at her house and sat down for a cup of tea and then we bought up what had been going on with Brett. She listened to what we had to say and asked why I had not asked mum about it while I was up there and again, I told her I was not comfortable discussing these things with mum as I had never received help from her before, only dismissiveness.

She asked me if I had been experiencing anything myself and I admitted that I had turned my back on it and was trying to live a normal life. She was in quiet thought for a while quietly sipping her tea, then she looked at me, took a deep breath and said to me, boy, this stuff is very powerful. If you have turned your back on it then it will jump to the next generation and make its choice again. She then said it seems like they have made another choice as you have turned your back on them; I don't like it when they pick on the kids. She told us she had seen other situations where kids were affected, and she was angry that this happens.

I just sat there dumbfounded. I did not know what to say or how to respond in any way. She told me that if things went bad with Brett to recite the Lord's Prayer. That is all she could tell me.

I have since discovered that the reason kids can be affected is that they are open. We are all born with spirituality. We are spiritual beings but along the way it is bred out of us by day to day life as well as the pace of life. It is also known as the quickening. Children on the other hand are pure and spiritual, they are still connected. Try this simple experiment next time you pick up a young baby. See where its eyes go when you pick them up and look at them. They are not looking at your face they are looking at your colours, your aura. That is how they originally recognise you. They are still spiritual and operate with colours and auras.

Well, we went home that night and after getting Brett bathed and into bed, Leanne and I sat down and had a good talk. This turn of events had us worried and it was at this time we decided to prepare to run back to Australia. We had been safe there before with nothing happening and we were sure we would be safe there again.

It was not something that could be done overnight, as we now had a house and contents to sell as well as the two cars. It was going to take a while.

From the time we made the decision to go back to Australia and put the house on the market, things with Brett started to go downhill. The housing market had crashed at the time and with all this spiritual activity going on, we just wanted to get out of the country again. His conversations with his 'friend' started to get heated like a child being scorned or teased and during the night he began waking up screaming and holding his stomach.

I just knew it was a spiritual episode he was going through so as Aunty Annie had told me, I began reciting the Lord's Prayer while holding Brett. This worked for a few weeks and as the episodes began getting more serious, the prayers no longer helped us. I again went to Aunty Annie seeking help. She told me this time to either get some holy water or use my urine to mark the cross on Brett's forehead as I recited the Lord's Prayer. This was really starting to get out of control, but we had some water blessed and kept it in the house. This was used many times as was the urine but as time progressed, we saw that they were becoming less effective. We could not sell the house quickly so just decided to rent it out so we could leave New Zealand.

The frequency and intensity of the episodes Brett was experiencing became much, much worse. We even witnessed him having arguments with his 'friend' during the day at this stage.

We held a garage sale and sold the entire contents of our house the following Saturday. It was a busy affair with people coming through all day, but we were glad that everything went. We had family around through the day to help but by the end of it all we were completely exhausted. It was late before we could finally relax. People who had bought the big items had to go away and get trailers to take their items away so it was well after dark before we could finally relax.

That night the intensity of what I call an attack on an innocent child, escalated to a point Brett was screaming in pain calling to his mother and myself to help him. Again, I tried the holy water and the urine while I recited the Lord's Prayer, but nothing worked.

I could not help my son. This was the most helpless and empty feeling I have ever felt, not only as a parent but as a person. We were panicking frantically, and I rang home to see if mum or dad knew where I could find Father Tate. I needed help and I needed it now. This is the ugly side of spirituality that I learnt to despise.

Mum told me that he was the priest at Hato Petera Private College on the North Shore, so I put an urgent call through to the school and they put me through to Father Tate. It was 3.00am, he answered the phone and I told him what was happening. Meanwhile Brett was still screaming and crying in the background along with his mother screaming for them to leave Brett alone. He told me to hold Brett and tell the entity to leave. Tell the entity you know what it is and to leave then recite the Lord's Prayer again he said. I did all of this while he listened on the phone. Brett calmed down and went straight to sleep in my arms. Poor bugger was exhausted. I spoke to Father Tate again and he told me to try and get to sleep and bring Brett to Te Unga Waka, a Marae in Auckland, first thing in the morning. Father Tate would conduct Sunday mass and he would then examine Brett to ascertain if he would have to carry out an exorcism on him. I told Leanne and we just looked at each other and thought what the hell is going on here.

We had only managed to get a couple of hours sleep so we were just as exhausted as Brett. We all had dealt with minimal sleep for the past few weeks with all these disturbances going on with Brett and then the garage sale etc. Life had been hectic for us all.

During the short sleep that I had, I found myself on the beach at Mitimiti. Well I say Mitimiti but the longer I was there the more I realised it was an alternate Mitimiti. The sunshine was warm, but it was a brighter whiter light than normal and the most beautiful thing I can remember is that you could just feel love. It was in the air that you were breathing, it was in the sea spray coming off the waves, it was everywhere. I began walking toward the rocks and two of my cousins walked up to me and said, we are glad you are awakening from your slumber. We are waiting for you to accept your role. We hugged and then I drifted before waking up back in my bed. When I woke up, I could still feel that amazing feeling of love. I have felt these many times since in different situations and they are among the most amazing euphoric sensations I have ever experienced.

We got up early in the morning after only a couple of hours sleep and readied ourselves to head to Te Unga Waka.

When we arrived there the service was just about to begin and as we were to go in, two of my cousins from Mitimiti walked in, the very same two I had seen only hours ago in my dream but in reality, I had not seen for years. I have not named them intentionally. They know who they are, and I thank you both. We sat down and I told them what was going on. They were so supportive, and I was glad they were there. We went into the service and afterwards Father Tate called us into another room. My cousins walked straight in with us and informed Pa that they were there to support us. He greeted them and thanked them as did we.

We spoke about what had happened and the fact that Brett had not been christened. We told him that we were planning to get out of New Zealand again as soon as we vacated the house. We had managed to rent the house out and were just waiting on settling a few things. He just kept examining Brett, looking all over him. He told us that the entity was still with Brett, it had attached itself to him.

He explained about the mana of the Rangatira and asked how I had been coping as he had helped me many times in my youth with issues of the same nature. I told him that I had turned my back on it. Once again, I was told the same story as was told by Aunty Annie, that as I had turned my back on this so-called gift it had proceeded to jump to the next generation and choose its next recipient. I was angry, I had a thousand emotions running through me at the time and dare I say it, I began to hate this gift. I had spent a large portion of my life running from this stuff and now it was affecting my son and he was just a baby.

Father Tate told me he would perform the exorcism this morning, in fact right away, but the following Sunday I was to present Brett to the Church at Hato Petera College and he would christen Brett after morning mass at the College. He told me to feel free to bring some family members.

Without any fanfare, Father Tate began the exorcism all conducted in Maori. Brett seemed as calm as can be throughout the whole process and just sat there looking all around Father Tate, looking at his colours. During this time, he looked so serene and content.

Afterwards, he told us that tonight the entity would be back. It will be its last fling. He handed me a vile of holy water and said, you know what to do with this. I took the vile, thanked him and we headed outside, and all had a chat before we headed off home. I told my cousins of the christening the following week and they both said they would come. I told them I had dreamt of them that morning and apart from a look of surprise, it was not mentioned again. They wished us the best and we headed for home.

We arrived home early in the afternoon and I called mum and dad to tell them what was going on with Brett, the exorcism, and the christening the following weekend. We also told them that we had rented the house as we were heading back to Australia.

There was genuine concern for Brett, Leanne and I and what we were going through and they said they would make it down the following weekend.

I decided to get some sleep, in preparation for the night, the last fling. We all got on to our big bed and slept for the afternoon, totally exhausted.

That night, as foretold, the entity did come back for its last fling. Brett was sound asleep, and it was the early hours of the morning. At first, he was asleep and then there were a few mumbled words and then all hell broke loose again.

Brett was screaming with tears rolling down his face grabbing his abdomen. I was swearing my head off telling it to just piss off. Leanne was asking it to leave, we were a real mess. It is not easy watching a child suffer and you are powerless to do anything about it.

Brett was still screaming for us to help him. Both his mother and I were frantic. I think this went on for about an hour, then as suddenly as it came, it was gone.

Brett was still asleep and just kept on sleeping sucking on the edge of his blanket.

Leanne and I stayed up all night but that was it, there was no more.

I rang Father Tate the following morning and told him the events of the night. He told me we should be ok now and the next thing to sort out was the christening.

The letting of the house went through that week and we had another busy schedule. We had the Christening on Sunday, then pack and move out to Leanne's parents on Monday then fly out of Auckland for Australia on Tuesday.

The week went very quickly. We still had people picking up stuff from the garage sale. One of the cars went but I was lucky to sell one to a workmate and we had it right up till we flew out.

As if all of this was not enough to deal with, we then had someone try to steal the last car we had to use till we left. This happened on the Friday night and it was one of the first times I was consciously aware of the warrior coming out from within me.

On this night there was hardly any furniture in the house as we had sold everything. We were staying in the house with the bare essentials that we had borrowed from family and friends so that we could clean the entire house before the tenants took possession.

We had had a long day and Leanne and Brett had fallen asleep on a mattress on the floor in the master bedroom. The Commonwealth Games was on TV, so I had a single mattress on the floor in the lounge with a small TV we had borrowed from my brother until we left for Australia.

I remember watching the games and looked at my watch and thought, 1.30am, I better hit the sack. I decided to sleep on the single mattress in the lounge rather than disturb Leanne and Brett. We had all been through a rough time and as they were sleeping, I did not want to ruin that.

The lights were already off, so I just turned off the TV and covered myself with a blanket and tried to get comfortable. I had no sooner got comfortable and trying to get to sleep when I heard the car door shut. The car was on the front lawn just outside the window.

I got up and crept over to the window, but I could not see anything as the house was elevated and I was looking down onto the roof of the car.

I snuck out through the front door and crept out onto the front deck peering around the corner of the sunroom. I could see a shape in the driver's seat hunched over, obviously trying to hotwire the car. The shadows from the large trees gave me cover to sneak down the footpath and sweep around behind the car on the lawn without making any noise. I approached the driver's door from the rear of the vehicle and could clearly see a person in the driver's seat still hunched over with his head down low on the driver's side. In one movement, I pulled the door open, grabbed a handful of hair and pulled him straight out of the car dragging him until I ran his head into the fence which was only about 2-3 metres away.

I then got him into an arm lock with one arm behind his back and I had my other arm up over his shoulder around his neck and locking his body back into mine so he could not get out of my grip. He was screaming that he was just looking for a place to sleep but just by looking in the car and seeing the wires he had pulled out from the dash you knew it was all just a lie. He was high as a kite and you could smell booze on him. I marched him along the front of the house and up the steps onto the front veranda. The door was still open from when I had come outside, so I yelled out to Leanne to call the Police. I had this guy restrained so tight with his face into the wall that he could not move. I was yelling out to Leanne from the veranda about what had happened, that it was an attempted car theft and I had apprehended him. This guy was begging me not to call the cops and I just told him to shut up. The Police said they were busy and would be 30 to 40 minutes. I told Leanne to hold the phone up so they can hear me. I yelled toward the phone, if that is the best you can do, I am just going to beat the crap out of this guy then he can go steal someone else's car and then told Leanne to hang up. I had only intended to say that to get some action by the Police but on hearing it, the guy then proceeded to piss his pants. I was pushing him away from my body so he would not piss on my feet, when he made his biggest mistake that night.

While I was bustling him around, he said, and I quote 'If you let me go, I won't come back and kill you and your family,' unquote.

In an instant I felt this power surge through me from within and unleash one hell of a beating on this guy. It was like I went to the back of my body and someone else just stepped in and dealt to this guy with no mercy. Leanne was screaming at me to stop, then all of a sudden three cop cars came to a screeching halt at the entrance to our street. I grabbed this guy by his blood matted hair and just dragged him down the front steps along the footpath and out the front gate where I was met by two officers. I released his hair and he just dropped onto the footpath screaming out obscenities at me. The cop asked what happened. I was back to myself at this stage and said he had fallen down the front steps. The guy was screaming I was a nutter and had beaten him up. The cop just looked at him and said no, you fell down the steps.

While they were arresting him, one of the cops took me aside and asked what really happened on the quiet. I told him how I had caught him inside the car and of the threat he had made against my family. He told me they would send extra patrols around our area for the next few nights just in case, but this guy will not be on the streets for quite a while.

I went back inside after the formalities and went back over the events in my head. I was trying to rationalise what had happened but the instant surge of power I experienced was like nothing I have ever known. The feeling of being set back in my own body while I virtually watched the events unfold before me. The speed and veracity of the beating being handed out was not of my doing, it was precise and practiced unlike anything I had seen before.

I know now that this was the warrior inside me being let out to protect me and ever since then, I have worked very hard to keep him under control. It actually shocked me to see this happen but ever since it has made me determined to keep him under control. I now understand that as part of my heritage, we once were warriors and that the warrior heart can and still does beat within us, but we need to be very careful in how we use it, or even worse unintentionally letting it out.

It is a very powerful part of our past but the best place for it is probably in the past in order for us to go forward in this new world.

On the Sunday morning we arrived at Hato Petera College Chapel for Brett's christening not really knowing how many of the family would turn up. We were just too busy to follow up with it. Mum, dad and the whole family were there and when Father Tate came out to greet us and saw everyone, he looked at me and said boy, you should have told me they were all coming. Tell them to wait here, we have to organise a powhiri for them. We all waited out on the road until the powhiri started, which was carried out by the Hato Petera culture group with finesse (the powhiri is a full Maori welcome).

We then proceeded into the Chapel for the christening as the school choir (that had just won a prestigious choir competition which embraced all islands in the South Pacific) performed some songs, in Maori, during and after the service. It was an amazing experience. It made the whole service feel so special. I noticed that throughout the whole christening ceremony, Brett was observing Pa Tate and his aural colours. When he wasn't being affected by all of this spiritual upheaval, Brett was always a happy child and it was so awesome to observe him when he was happy.

The christening was an awesome service accompanied by more beautiful music by the choir. At the completion of the service we all made our way outside and chatted with Pa Tate, other members of the family or students from the school. Father Tate came and greeted the family and used it as an opportunity to catch up with everyone, especially mum and dad, along with Leanne, Brett and me. My cousins who had attended the exorcism the weekend before were in attendance and it was a good opportunity to also catch up with them and again thank them for their support.

Some of the students from the school also came and introduced themselves and we all chatted about the service. They told us Father Tate had rushed back into the Chapel to organise a powhiri for us and he had told them that they had special guests from the far north coming in to have a family member christened. As they were in a boarding school it was a good opportunity to catch up with them and for them it was also a treat to see whanau. My father had also been a student of this College as had many other people from our area. It was a very highly regarded Maori College in the day.

Mum and dad were staying with my sister Georgina and her husband Ron, so after we had finished catching up with everyone and thanking Father Tate, we all headed to their house for a coffee and to spend a bit of time as we were flying back to Australia in 2 days' time.

We left later in the afternoon and headed back to our place for the final night before we vacated it. Again, we were exhausted. I don't think Leanne and I even had dinner that night, she just fed Brett and we all fell asleep.

The following day we packed up the car, signed the last papers and handed over the house keys to the letting agency. It was time to begin another chapter in our lives and we headed out to Leanne's parents to spend the last night and have one more of Leonie's awesome dinners.

Brett enjoyed the last night with his grandparents and you could hear his laughter throughout the house all evening. It was awesome to hear him enjoying some quality time with his grandparents.

After the events of the past few weeks it was like we were waking up from a bad dream and I could not wait to get out of New Zealand and go back to what I considered to be a safe place, Western Australia. We had moved home at Christmas 1990 and headed back to Australia March 1994.

The whole experience of the past 6 months had completely worn us down. We were no longer able to contend with the constant episodes we could not comprehend or find any closure to. We put on a brave face and had told everyone we were going back to Australia because we loved it so much. In all honesty we did love being in Australia, but we were not going to tell anyone we were once again running from what was my heritage because if we did not understand it, I didn't think anyone else would either. I had in the past tried to address these issues but with no guidance or assistance, so our best option was again to leave New Zealand. So that is exactly what we did. At the airport, the morning we were once again to fly out I was asked if we would ever come back home to live again. The answer was no. After all we had recently been through, I don't think there could be any other answer to that question.

CHAPTER 7

Back to Australia

It was Tuesday morning and we were up and off to the airport early as we were booked on a mid-morning flight. We said our goodbyes to family and friends who were at the airport to see us off. As I boarded the plane, I felt the familiar sensation of a weight once again being lifted from my shoulders. We flew out of Auckland for Melbourne. We decided to stay with Jack and Cindy for a week on route to Perth so they could meet Brett and we could catch up.

On the fourth night we were there I had a really powerful and disturbing dream. I did not understand all of it but recognised bits and pieces, especially an overwhelming feeling of death. I woke up feeling apprehensive and not being too sure of what was going on. I described what had happened with Leanne and decided to ring home.

I rang home and mum answered the telephone. I asked who had passed away as I had felt it in my sleep. It was Whina Cooper. Whina was a very well respected Panguru kuia and local. She was a real pioneering Maori woman who had faced many obstacles in her life but was known nationally for her Maori land march in 1975, from Te Hapua in the North to Parliament in the country's capital Wellington.

This protest had shed a lot of light on the plight of Maori land issues and gained so much support from Maori country wide as well as pakeha anti-racism groups that it could not be ignored. The plight of Maori land issues was bought to the fore and was acknowledged by government, thereby forcing the issue dealing with and addressing many land issues which were being dealt with at the time and also in years to come.

For the first time I realised that this so-called 'gift' had followed me to Australia. I was a bit apprehensive about it all at first, but I thought to myself, we are going back to Western Australia (WA). It has never followed me there. It was my way of rationalising it I suppose. It helped to keep my mind off it.

We headed back to Perth three days later and when we arrived, I just relaxed. There was no longer any apprehension over what had transpired days earlier and I was able to completely relax and focus on what we needed to do.

We stayed in Perth for a few days and bought a car and trailer then picked up some tea chests we had sent over from New Zealand to start again in Western Australia.

With the trailer packed we once again headed back to Kalgoorlie to look for work and settle down again.

In Kalgoorlie we caught up with many friends whom we had made on our first trip here. It was such a blast seeing them all again.

We did the hard yards for the next year or so with me working away and getting home to see Leanne and Brett on every occasion I could. Brett was so excited to see me when I could get home and would never leave my side. It was a good break for his mum and I genuinely loved having my son with me. Life for us was very busy and with everything going on I didn't even have time to think about my so-called 'gift'. I just knew I was glad that we were safe, for now anyway.

At one stage Leanne wanted to see how things would turn out for us in the future so she decided she would go to see a clairvoyant. After my reading with Graham back in New Zealand, I was not so apprehensive and did not actually mind.

There was a clairvoyant visiting from Perth, her name was Chanty. Leanne made a booking for herself after I had got home from work as I was now working just outside of Kalgoorlie. We all had dinner and while Leanne went to her reading I looked after Brett and put him to bed.

Brett went down without an issue and about half an hour later Leanne arrived home. She walked in and I asked how her reading went. She walked in and said tongue in cheek, that was a waste of time. All she could talk about was your family. I laughed and she said she got a bit of what she wanted to know but Chanty just kept on going on about my family and this powerful chief. I sat there listening to her and I must admit, it really got my attention. Leanne told me that Chanty was a really nice person who made you really feel at ease.

She looked at me and said, you really need to go and see her. This stuff was all about you, that chief and your family; it must be important. I thought about it and decided I would go and see her. The reading I had with Graham in New Zealand had broken down many issues I had with going to a medium for a reading. Leanne made the booking for me the following day and I was to go 2 days later. This time around, I wasn't worried at all. There was actually no fear, no apprehension. I was actually looking forward to it.

On the night of my reading I was completely relaxed which surprised me. I got home from work, had a shower and dinner with the family then helped get Brett ready for bed. I gave him a big hug and kisses as I knew he would be in bed by the time I got home.

I went to the appointment and even though I had never met Chanty, I was in good spirits and hoped she could give me as much information as she gave Leanne.

I arrived at the address and knocked on the door. Chanty opened the door and welcomed me in. I walked in and she continued to hold the door open. I carried on into the room then looked back at her still holding the door and gave her a look as if to say, what is going on, I am already inside. She just smiled at me and said, I see you have bought your entourage and went on to describe the energy of the Maori Chief that had followed me in along with some others who were also Maori, saying they looked like warriors. She was holding the door open until they were in the room and then closed it.

We sat down for the reading when Chanty asked me if I had been to many readings. I told her that this was only the second reading I had ever had and gave her some background information about how I came to be at the first reading.

She looked at me and asked me if I knew what was behind all of this activity. I told her I had no clue. She kept looking up beside me and behind me, describing who she could see. She told me that his energy was a very powerful and beautiful energy and that he stood beside me in full Maori dress and with a tattoo all over his face. The others were dressed in Maori dress too, but she said it was clear that he was the head of the group. I told her the facial tattoos would be his moko and she said he was nodding. She then continued to tell me that in his day he was a very powerful and respected figure. He was also known to be very hard but also very fair in his decisions and that he lived a very long life. He was one hundred years old when he died. She asked for his name and he replied with the keeper. At the time I did not know what the keeper meant so she asked again. He replied explaining that he was the keeper of the tribe. Much of the time she would look directly at me, then look to my side then back to me and talk to me. You are hard to wake from your slumber she said to me. He tells me he has been trying to get your attention since you were a boy.

She then said to me have you ever thought to yourself after you had been through a certain situation, wow I'm lucky to survive that, or wow I should be dead. I sat there and thought for a little bit then replied to her, yeah maybe once or twice. She started laughing her head off and told me that she was laughing because they were all laughing saying it was much more than that. To be honest, I knew it was way more than that I was just not going to say. Even I know I was out of control in my youth. I was trying to resist something I could not see and the only way I could find to get relief from what I was dealing with was to run amok. As I said earlier in this book, I had nowhere to turn for help. I was on my own, so I dealt with it the only way I knew how. To lash out.

She continued, the reason you made it through all of those situations was that you were being protected. This Chief tells me they have been watching over you to make sure nothing happens to you. There is something you are meant to do during your lifetime, and they are watching out for you so that you do what you are supposed to do. You have much to learn to do the thing they want you to do as this will be your last time here (on earth) she told me while looking up and around me. I sat there in silence and thought about all the things I had got away with, car accidents, speeding, brawls and just doing stupid shit and managing to come out the other side unscathed. I believed that there could actually be some merit in what she was saying.

She then went back to me being hard to wake up and that the keeper had told her that on many occasions they had tried to get my attention and had failed but that when the time was right, I would awaken. She asked me to be more open and to listen to my body more. She even told me what was behind the episode with Brett in New Zealand and I had not mentioned it to her. She was told that I had turned my back on them, so they actually chose someone from the next generation of our family to carry out my role if I did not wake up. That person was Brett and they were also using him to try to wake me up. I must admit, they got my attention but what a way to do it. I was not really sure if I could accept what I had been told but, again, it somehow really started to make sense to me although I still sat there dumbfounded at hearing all of this.

The explanation she gave me was that they do not see him as a child, that is an earthly trait. They see the soul inside the body and that soul can be very old and could have been here on previous occasions. On one hand, I still did not understand how this all worked yet I was not disputing any of it. On the other hand, this was all beginning to give me a different perspective on the past events and makes sense in a confusing sort of way.

She ended the reading thanking the keeper for his presence and at the same time she reiterated that there was nothing to fear but fear itself which for some reason, made absolute sense to me. She then said to me, things will settle down, you will be working back in town soon. I had not even asked about that but it was something I really wanted to happen so I could be back at home with my family.

We sat and chatted about what had transpired, and I must admit, to me it actually seemed to shed a lot of light on my past. Well it did to me anyway.

I thanked Chanty and headed home knowing Leanne would be waiting up to see how it went. Again, Chanty held the door open as I left to allow for my 'entourage' to exit behind me. When I got home, I went through everything with Leanne and the funny thing was, she actually agreed with me that a lot of what had been said actually made sense. For the first time in my life I actually had a grasp on the spiritual happenings in my life thanks to Chanty and again thanks to Leanne.

After this life went on for us as normal for a while. I had transferred back to Kalgoorlie and was living at home. I then got approached to go to work for another company in Coolgardie which meant even less travelling. I decided to jump at the opportunity even though I really wanted to go back to underground mining as it was better money and more days off for family time.

Seven months later I went back to working underground working 4 days on and 4 days off. By this stage we had bought a house in the town of Coolgardie. We were lucky as it was a new home. It was a big house and we got it at a good price as the couple that built it split up. The house had never been lived in, but the yards needed a lot of work as they had not been touched and it did not have any fences.

Over the next 2 years I did a lot of work on the place, levelling off the block, getting lawns established and getting fences built. We decided to build a patio and garage which was a big task in itself, but it was well worth it.

We also decided we needed a dog as Brett really wanted a dog since his last dog Pipi had to be euthanised with a broken hip. We think she must have been hit by a car.

We planned to go down to Wundowie just east of Perth and buy a cocker Spaniel. We had a Spaniel several years earlier and even took him back to New Zealand. Ziggy was so protective of Brett it was uncanny, and he would always be company for Brett when he went wandering and let us know where they both were. When we decided to come back to Australia, Ziggy was too old to make the trip, so I gave him to my cousin as a mate for her son.

Anyway, on my next break we decided we were going to get a dog. We all went to bed early. I wanted to get away by 4am, as it was a 6-hour drive to Perth to look for another Spaniel. We got up the next morning, Brett was all excited, and we packed a few things into the car and headed off. We drove all the way to Southern Cross, which was about an hour and a half away, then stopped for fuel and a bite to eat at the truck stop. I bought the local paper the Kalgoorlie Miner and looked under pets for sale. We had been keeping an eye on the paper for the last 2 weeks and nothing came up. However, this time there was a cocker Spaniel in Kalgoorlie, 18 months old and free to a good home. I waited till we had finished breakfast then rang the number. It was a private number and she told us he was a trained Blue Roan Spaniel. I had a quick talk with Leanne, then told the lady we were interested and would turn around and head back to Kalgoorlie. She told us she would keep him until we had been to see him, so we jumped back in the car, turned around and headed back to Kalgoorlie.

We found the address in Kalgoorlie with no worries and as soon as we saw the dog, Leanne and Brett were all over him. He had to be the most energetic cocker Spaniel I had ever seen. We laughed at how his stubby tail was going at 100 mile an hour and we thought he was going to fly away. The lady explained how it was her son's dog and he just did not have time to spend with it, so it was time to let him go. She also had a Spaniel of her own and both dogs would play tug of war with an old sock all over the furniture. It was hilarious to watch. We were stoked and put Georgie in the car with us where he snuggled up to Brett in the back seat while we headed home. Georgie became a real part of the family in a very short amount of time and was a great dog to have around. The only time he barked was at 5 o'clock, his dinner time.

Georgie and Brett became inseparable. Everywhere Brett went, along went Georgie with his tail spinning like a propeller and it was so funny to watch. They would go for walks in the bush with Georgie coming home covered in dust and bindii, what a mess.

With Georgie to keep Brett company on many of his adventures, I found I had a bit of spare time on my hands. Sunday mornings became the neighbourhood kids' day. I would wake up on Sunday mornings and if I was not off working, there would be all these young kids outside our front gate waiting for me to wake up. They said I was the only dad that would go out for rides with them. Brett and I would mount our bikes and we were off, me on my Honda with all these young kids under ten on their peewee 50 bikes. It was good fun. There were so many bush tracks around town you could ride for miles.

I finally got around to concreting the floor in the big shed. When this was done Leanne and I decided one night that I would build a hairdressing salon inside the shed so she could work from home, with the flexibility of having time with Brett when she wanted or when it was required. It ticked all the boxes for us as I was still working underground on a rotating roster, so she did need some flexibility with her work.

I did most of the work myself but had some help from friends. My brother Harry who was still living in Kalgoorlie also helped out when he could and when my sister Cindy and her husband Jack visited from Wonthaggi, Jack also pitched in to help get it finished which I was very grateful for.

When the building was complete, we needed to find plant and equipment for the shop and Leanne needed to find a supplier for products. We headed off to Perth for a week to sort it out and this was the weekend that Princess Diana was killed in Paris. It was all over the media.

We managed to find everything we needed, Leanne had secured a supplier and I bought a tandem trailer with gates so we could get everything back to Coolgardie.

We had everything fitted into the salon when we got back. It still took quite a few weeks to finally finish it all off with power, water, phone plumbing etc., then we had the signwriting and such to do.

I was so glad when we were close to opening. It was like seeing light at the end of the tunnel after 5 months building. It was impressive with a classy black and white finish and black latticework on a white ceiling. Everyone commented on how nice it was to have a fancy modern hairdressing salon in town as the closest hair salon was 40 kms away in Kalgoorlie.

We were into our last week of preparation before opening and everything was running along smoothly. I went back to work after my days off and Leanne was sorting out bank accounts and paperwork for the salon as well as organising advertising for the opening day. Everything was going well until we got a phone call that was about to change the course of our lives, we just didn't know it yet.

CHAPTER 8

Farewell to My Father

We were into December of 1997. Things were going well with Leanne's Hairdressing Salon and she would be opening the doors later in the week for business.

I arrived home from work that night and Leanne came running out of the house. I knew something was wrong by her body language and the fact that she was all emotional. She rushed out to the side of the road to meet me and told me my father had passed away earlier on in the day from a heart attack.

I rang home straight away and spoke with one of my sisters. The family had all begun racing home once they heard the news. Dad owned the local bus company and she explained that mum and dad with their moko Candice had just returned from a shopping day in Kaitaia when they stopped in to pick up a bus which was in Broadwood for maintenance. Normally any moko usually rode back in the bus with poppa to the farm, but that day nanna told Candice to hop into the car with her to go home.

After dad picked up the bus, the locals said the horn was blaring and it is believed dad suffered a massive heart attack as the bus came down the hill. The bus then veered off the road and into a drain near the school. Mum could not be informed about the accident until she got home. When she got the phone call, she drove back to the scene.

In hindsight, I was thankful that the accident did not happen with anybody else on board and my niece had gone with mum in the car.

I hung up the phone and said to Leanne, I have got to get home. The opening for the salon was in 2 days so we decided that Brett and I would go home, and Leanne would stay to open her salon.

My passport had expired so I had to ring the New Zealand Embassy in Sydney, then ring home again to get a Death Certificate sent to the Embassy. They told me they would send a fax to the Perth airport to let me out of the country, but I could not return until I had a valid passport. I could not book flights home until the fax had been sent, so Brett and I packed our bags loaded them into the car and headed to Perth.

Leanne sorted things out while we were on the road. We got to Perth 6 hours later and I rang Leanne straight back. The fax had been sent and she had booked both me and Brett to fly out that night. The Embassy had also organised for immigration officials to meet us when we landed in Auckland with passport renewal papers. We boarded our flight and headed for Auckland.

Brett was actually really good to travel with. He was content and he just thought he was going on a trip with dad, after all he was only six years old then.

During the flight I never slept a wink. All I could see was a picture of the homestead in my mind. It had burned down 10 years earlier but that was still the vision I was seeing. I had to get home.

We arrived in Auckland in the early hours of the morning with other family members all flying in within 2 hours of our arrival. The bus that was supposed to pick us up never arrived, so we were frantically trying to find vehicles. I rang Leanne's parents and they were kind enough to run a car up to the airport for us to head north.

As it turned out we had more family members coming into Auckland in the early afternoon, so we all decided to wait for them and head up together. We ended up with a convoy of vehicles leaving Auckland early in the evening. We headed north and I asked Cousin Wayne to drive our car as I had not slept for two full days at this stage. When we got up onto the gravel roads at Mangamuka he was not confident of driving those roads, so I took over.

We arrived at Mitimiti at around 1 am and proceeded straight to the Marae. There were already many people there and after a welcoming powhiri we were allowed into the Whare Hui where dad was lying in state.

As is customary, we went around and greeted my family, working our way up to the cask where my mother sat weeping.

I don't know why but as I hongi with each of my family members, I was calling them by the nicknames we used for each other when we were kids. Each time it resulted in them laughing and cracking up.

I got up to the coffin and went to hug my mother. She embraced me with tears in her eyes but laughing and said to me, you have not changed, you still make us laugh.

I was told later that a visiting elder said to his son, how disrespectful of me going in to make everyone laugh at a tangi. He said to his father, that is just Ronnie, that is how he always is. It's not him being disrespectful at all its just him being him.

I have used laughter to hide many emotions over the years, fear, sadness or even hatred.

It was a mechanism I developed years earlier when I was facing the scary side of spirituality and I had no one I could talk to or open up to. In a sense, I don't think I use it anymore but these days I laugh more for the sake of laughing. It is good for your soul. I have faced my fears and no longer require a protective mechanism as it were. I have moved past that.

The tangi was a large affair with many people coming to pay their respects to my father. It was during this time, when people were expressing their sorrow and thanks to my father, that we became aware of the fact that he had been helping so many people with gifts of money, food or services to help them out. We sat there listening to many stories of how our father had helped all of these people and we did not even know. Mum didn't know either for that matter, she was as surprised as us kids were.

It actually made me feel very humble hearing how dad had helped these people just because he could. I had now heard of a side of my father that made me so very proud of him. I had lost respect for my father years before for reasons I won't go into but, in short, I felt he was trying to buy my favour at the time and I have never been for sale, so it did not sit right with me at all at the time. These stories of how he helped so many actually regained my respect for him. At the time, after hearing all of these stories, I thought to myself I wish I could have forgiven my dad before he passed. As I found out further along my journey, I was lucky enough to be able to forgive him even after his death.

It was nice to meet up with cousins that I had not seen for a long time but it's a shame this mostly happens at weddings and funerals. I caught up with so many people it was awesome. I had to laugh to myself one day. I was sitting with Brett having lunch on the Marae when he turned to me and said, hey dad, what are all the aboriginals doing here?

I had a chuckle and replied, Brett they are not aboriginals, they are Maori's. Well dad, what are they doing here then he said. I had to explain that they were all his cousins and relations. He asked me why they were darker than us if we are Maori's, which I thought was a pretty good question for a 6-year-old. I replied to him with we were born in the daytime son and left it at that.

You have to understand that Brett was bought up in Australia in the Goldfields of Western Australia. The indigenous people or what we refer to as Tangata Whenua (people of the land) of that country are aboriginal and he was used to going to school with them and playing with them and naturally assumed the dark-skinned Maori were aboriginal. Such an innocent perspective by a child, made without malice or prejudice. I took a mental note to teach him about his heritage so that he would never be lost like that again. I wanted him to know who he was, where he was from and where his roots were. It is innately our grounding.

I watched him that afternoon how he went and played with all the cousins around the place and had a fat ole time. It reminded me of the days we spent on the Marae when I was younger.

The night before the funeral, as was customary, the walking stick went around the Whare Hui where everyone in the room related who they were and how they knew dad or how they were related.

Some of the stories that came out had us all in stitches while others told how he had helped them, again showing another side of our father that we were just becoming aware of.

In the early hours of the morning, I saw my Tupuna all standing out in front of the Whare Hui waiting. I knew that they were here to guide my father to the other side and unlike the first time I witnessed it in Pukekohe at my nana's tangi where I was gripped by fear, I now felt comfort and peace in knowing my father will be looked after.

The breaking of dawn signalled the beginning of the new day in which we had to say goodbye to dad and lay him to rest.

Everyone awoke that morning and preparations for the funeral were well underway just after daybreak. Breakfast was served and the wharekai was cleaned up before the final service was carried out by Father Tate in the church Hato Hemi. There were actually two priests in attendance at dad's service and Pa Tate bought it up during the service. Bully was a very important man he said humorously, so important that he has two priests to conduct his service. It was a bit of tongue in cheek which we all new Pa Tate for and everyone chuckled at the banter.

We were sitting in the church for the service which was predominantly conducted in the Maori language. For those of you who can properly pronounce the words such as whakapapa and Whakatane, you will understand how funny I thought it was when during the service, my son Brett taps me on the shoulder and whispers to me, hey dad, why are they swearing while they're prayering. I almost lost it. Not the best thing to do in the middle of a funeral but it was so innocent, and he was so serious when he asked that question, I just wanted to burst out laughing. I could understand why he came out with that comment but yeah not appropriate. Again, I took a mental note to teach him his heritage and culture.

I actually thought to myself, he has come up with some pretty good questions for a 6-year-old and I could understand why he would have had that point of view. I have to blame myself for not taking the time to teach him his culture and heritage at an earlier stage but under the circumstances it was a big ask.

I have since taught him many things in this regard, as it is his right and for his benefit that he knows it. That way he knows who he is and where he comes from. I just hope he remembers it in the years ahead.

The service was really good, and Father Tate reiterated the importance of our family having rangatira in our family line on both sides and the handing down of the mana. He was staring straight at me when he was talking of this matter and to be honest, I felt a little trapped. I averted my gaze away from him and tried to understand the ramifications of what he was saying. I had turned to Pa many times in my youth with spiritual problems and he had spoken about this with me in the past, but I continued to ignore what he was saying preferring to think to myself this has nothing to do with me and trying to move along. What could they want with me?

Originally there was supposed to be a logging truck come down to carry the cask to the Urupa (graveyard) but all us boys got together and said no, we wanted to carry dad to his final resting place.

After the service all of my brothers and my sisters became pall bearers. It was quite a walk out the entrance to the Marae and up the hill to the Urupa. We were carrying dad along and all of a sudden some of our cousins we had grown up with came along side us and said to us, let us share your load bro. They took our places as pall bearers to give us a break and then later on we changed back again.

It was one of the most emotional times in my life as we returned my father to the ground from where he came. I stood silently thanking him for bringing me into this world and raising me to be who I am.

I still go to see him and have a chat every time I go home.

That afternoon, after saying our goodbyes to those who had to leave and then having a meal (kai) in the wharekai, Brett had gotten worn out and was really tired. Mum had said she needed to go home for a rest, and she left straight after the meal. Not long after this, I gathered Brett and took him back to the house.

Brett and I had been sleeping in one of the bedrooms, so I took him in there and put him to bed. He was worn out and was sucking on the silk edge of his blanket already asleep as I lay him down.

I left the room and went out to have a cup of tea with mum. We sat and chatted for a while and then I put some washing of Brett's in the washing machine. Mum told me to go back to the Marae and she would keep an eye on Brett and bring him back down when she went back down. I told her ok, I would just check on Brett before I went.

I went into the room and he was fast asleep, so I got changed and headed back down to the Marae for drinks.

Mum rang the Marae about an hour later and told me to go home.

Straight away I thought that something had happened to Brett.

I got home and Brett was up with nanna holding him in the kitchen. I walked in and asked, what is wrong? She told me what had happened.

She said she went up to the bedroom and walked in. Brett was sitting there with his eyes wide open and his arms outstretched. She then went over to him and said, are you alright Brett? He looked at her and said, nanna, poppa just came to say hooray to me and then he floated out over the sea. She picked Brett up and carried him out to the kitchen and called me.

We are all born with our spirituality intact. It has not been bred out of us at this stage of life and we are innocent souls who see everything. As I explained earlier with seeing your colours, infants are still able to see spirit when they are young because they have not yet been affected by what we call everyday life. With Brett I thought that this may have been a one off but that was going to be proven wrong on the journey ahead.

We went back down to the Marae that night but did not stay that long. We went down as a sign of respect then went home again and I went to bed with Brett, he was exhausted.

We stayed for a few more days after the funeral and I received a call from New Zealand Immigration saying my passport was ready to pick up in Auckland. I was impressed for the quick turnaround and thankful for how much they did to assist me considering the circumstances.

We went back to Auckland the day before we flew back to Perth to collect my new passport, drop off the car to Leanne's parents and to stay the night before we left. After all, Brett was their grandson too.

Brett was all excited when we arrived at Leanne's parents that afternoon. He was being spoilt and enjoying his time with nana Leonie and grandad Ron. While we were there, they gave me a company profile to look over. It was a waste to energy company that had its roots in New Zealand. I had a quick look through the prospectus and packed it in my bag to take home with me as they said I could have it. We spent the rest of the evening eating a lovely dinner and talking about what was going on with them as well as what we were up to in Australia. Brett had a great night with nanna and granddad, and they were so happy to have some time with him before we left.

The following day we had breakfast with Ron and Leonie. Our flight wasn't until mid-morning so we could take our time and not have to rush.

When we got to the airport, we had some family and friends there to see us off and Brett made the most of his last hours with his grandparents. We finally said our final farewells to everyone and boarded the plane with the familiar sensation of a weight being lifted from my shouldersonce again. We were on our way back to Perth, Western Australia.

CHAPTER 9

Western Australia Safe Haven No More

Brett and I landed in Perth late in the evening after leaving New Zealand. We were exhausted so I booked a motel in Perth for the night. I rang Leanne and told her what we were up to and that we would see her the following day.

Early the next morning we left Perth to avoid the morning traffic and drove the 6 hours back to Coolgardie still tired. We got home around midday and Leanne had clients in the salon, so Brett and I unpacked the car. Brett knew he had a surprise in store and unloaded the car in record time. Unfortunately, he just dumped everything inside the front door on the floor because he was so excited about his surprise. His mother then took a break from her work and we gave Brett his Xmas present a day early. We had bought Brett a new XR70cc Honda for Xmas, as he had outgrown the 50cc bike he already had. I had raced into Kalgoorlie to pick it up before we flew home for dad's tangi. We had shown it to Brett before we flew out as we did not know if my passport would be renewed in time to get home for Xmas. Thanks again to the New Zealand Immigration Office, we had made it. We had lots of bush tracks around us back then so we could ride for miles with no worries. We spent hours out there riding our bikes, exploring and finding jumps for Brett to try out his new bike on.

That afternoon when Leanne finished work, she cooked dinner and waited for us to get home. We arrived home just before dark and then we washed up and all sat down for a meal. Over dinner we told Leanne how our trip home went. I explained to her that it had been a bit of a culture shock for Brett in the beginning, but he had adjusted while we were there and actually enjoyed meeting all his cousins. She told us her salon had been busy since she had opened the doors and it was going well. The locals had supported her from day one with bookings coming in at a steady rate.

Brett and I were still tired from all the travelling and the excitement of getting his new motorbike, so after the dishes were done, we all went to bed.

That night I had a really strange dream. I dreamt I was back in the old homestead which had burned down in 1987. It was as if I had been taken back in time to the old homestead. It was just so surreal, and I could have sworn that I was actually there. The one thing I really did notice was that old familiar feeling of peace that I feel today when I go home even though the old house is not there anymore.

In my dream I walked through the front door and into the front porch which doubled as a bedroom then entered the large main lounge area. The light was on in the porch but not in the lounge. I walked into the lounge and noticed the TV was on but all that was coming up on the screen was snow. I could sense dad was in the room but could not see him as it was so dark, so I blindly felt around until I found a seat and sat down and stared at the TV screen. I don't know how long I sat watching snow interference on the screen before another person came in through the front door. Every time I looked up another person had stepped just inside the lounge door and stopped. The light in the front porch was behind them so they just looked like a dark silhouette and I could not tell who they were. This went on a number of times, twelve in all I counted.

They all walked in and each found a seat to sit down. We all sat there staring at the snow on the TV screen without saying a word, when all of a sudden someone got up, walked over and turned off the TV then walked to the side hallway and turned on the light switch.

I looked around the room at the people who had entered the room and they were all Maori Chiefs just sitting in silence.

I heard someone start to speak in Maori and turned around to see my father standing and addressing the gathering. Usually I can only pick up bits and pieces of the Maori language but found that I could understand what he was saying as if it were English.

He was welcoming everyone to this meeting of the circle of Chiefs and ran through the agenda for the meeting ahead. When he had finished working through the agenda, he introduced me as his son and asked me to stand and acknowledge our guests. I was a bit shell shocked to say the least. I stood up and dad started to speak again. I looked over at him and I remember he was mid-sentence and I could not help myself, I just burst out, hey this cannot be real, you are dead.

At this point I remember waking up with a jolt, sitting upright in bed and found myself staring down the hallway in disbelief at what I had just experienced.

At this point I need to explain the outlay of our house, so you get the whole picture of what was about to happen.

Our house was a 4-bedroom house and Brett's room was the furthest one away down the hallway toward the other end of the house. Lying in bed we could look down the hallway into his room and see him in his bed. It was very handy on nights where he was unsettled.

Anyway, like I said I woke up with a jolt sitting bolt upright in bed and found myself looking down the hallway towards Brett's room.

As I stared, I saw Brett stir in bed, then he rolled out of his bed and began walking up the hallway toward our bedroom. I watched him as he walked into our bedroom before he walked around to my side of the bed and stood next to me. What he said next just blew me out of the water.

Why did you have to go and say that for dad?

I sat there dumbfounded at what I heard, and then he repeated it, why did you have to go and say that for dad? I replied, say what

Brett? It was at this time that I realised he was still asleep. I grabbed a hold of him and lifted him into our bed. He was out cold and fast asleep. I sat there thinking to myself, could he really have been in my dream with me? I was still dog tired, so I just acknowledged the dream, put it to the side and it was not long before I drifted off to sleep again.

The next morning after Leanne and I woke up I told her what had happened and then Brett woke up. I asked him if he remembered what had happened during the night and he just said he saw me talking with poppa and that I said something, and poppa left.

I asked him if he had seen poppa since the time in the house at Mitimiti after the funeral and he said he had. He told me that he had seen poppa in Auckland before we left and again in Perth in the motel when I was asleep.

I sat there not knowing what to think or say. Leanne just gave me a funny look and there wasn't much more we could say or do, except that we knew this was the first time ever that anything spiritual had followed us from New Zealand to Western Australia.

Funnily enough, considering all that had happened to us in the past, I was not scared of the happenings. I do not know if it was because I knew it was my dad or the fact that our son had been hurt by supernatural things in the past but this time, he showed no fear. I suppose I thought that if he showed no fear then I had no reason to show any fear either.

I had only been home from New Zealand for a day when I got a call from mum. Her youngest brother Uncle Kiri Ngawaka had passed away. I told her I would not be coming back for the tangi as I had only arrived home the previous day but asked where it was to be held. She told me the tangi would be held at Nga Hau e Wha Marae in Pukekohe. Knowing how big that side of our whanau is I told mum I would arrange for all the vegetables to be supplied for the tangi.

I rang an old school mate, Todd Nicoll, in Pukekohe. Todd is one of a handful of friends that I have known since Primary School. He was also the best man at my wedding. He had his own transport business back at this stage, so I told him what was going on and asked him to organise bins of vegetables, everything that was in season and get them delivered to the Marae. He told me that would not be a problem and I just told him to send me the bill. Well I did not hear back from Todd for a few days, but I was speaking to my brother John on the phone and asked if the vegetables had arrived. He told me that Todd had sent a truck out loaded with bins of vegetables and by account, it was on the day after I had called him. I waited a few more days for an invoice but it never came, so I gave Todd another call. I need to give you a bit of background information at this stage so that you understand how this all transpired.

When I went to High School in Pukekohe for the first 4 months of my third form year, I was in the so-called nerd class as we were all the so-called brainy people.

Most of the kids in my class were the children of market gardeners in the district, (Pukekohe back then was famous for its vegetables as it was very fertile land thanks to volcanic activity a long time ago). Out of the whole class there were only a handful of us that were involved in sports which actually meant we were not considered nerds. I was involved in rugby and lifesaving. Anyway, I never treated anyone else in our class as nerds and got them into many parties just because they came with me. Do not ask me why, I did not see myself as anything special, but I can still remember turning up to parties and they were all outside because they were not allowed in, then I would tell them to come with me and we would get straight in. I just knew a lot of people and that is all I put it down to and never thought anymore of it.

Anyway, as it turns out, Todd rang around to the market gardeners that he knew that I knew, and it turned out that the sons and daughters of those families that I went to school with were now running the operations. He told them what he needed and what they were for and then told them that he was doing it for me. Todd told me that as soon as he told them they were for me, they told him to stop around and pick them up, no charge, but next time I was back in New Zealand I was to come back to Pukekohe and catch up with them. That is why he had not sent an invoice and just had not got around to calling back as he was so busy. It was nice to think that after all those years, old friends still remember you and pitch in to help out.

I was just so thankful for the vegetables to help with my uncle Kiri's tangi.

It was several days later that I had my next vision. I say vision because I was not asleep. I was on one of my rare days off and was actually relaxing for a change. The trip to Mitimiti and then going straight back to work once I was home had worn me down a tad. I was in the lounge playing PlayStation Tomb Raider one. It was all the rage back then. All of a sudden, I heard this ringing in my head. It wasn't in my ears; it was in my mind. I stopped playing and lay back in the beanbag I was in and had a stretch and shaking my head trying to shake the ringing out of my head. I just sat there for a while and then all of a sudden, my father appeared before me. He was covering his face, but I knew it was him. I sat there looking at him and I actually asked what was wrong. He dropped his hands enough for me to see his eyes. I looked into his eyes and in those eyes, I could read him like a book. All of a sudden all of this emotion came flooding through me. He then covered his eyes again and I said it's alright dad, I forgive you and I love you. His hands came down below his eyes again and I repeated myself it's alright dad, I forgive you and I love you. This time his hands came down to his sides, tears were rolling down my face and I saw tears running down his. He looked at me, smiled, gave me a nod and turned and moved away.

As I mentioned earlier, I had fallen out with my father years before and had lost respect for him due to reasons I will not go into.

I just realised that I had been given the opportunity to make peace with my father and was lucky enough to be able to do it even after he had passed on. Though my loss of respect was not hateful or spiteful, I felt like a huge weight had been lifted from me. I actually did regain respect for my father when I heard all of the stories at his tangi of how he had helped many people that we were not even aware of. It was such an emotional experience for me that I was still crying several minutes later when Leanne came into the house for her lunch break from the salon. I told her what had happened, and she came over and gave me a hug. The experience was so powerful and emotional for me that even as I write this on my computer almost 23 years after the event, it brings a tear to my eyes. This was the first event in my spiritual journey where I had been so affected by what I was experiencing that the effects of it have changed the way I live my life in that aspect.

I find that now when someone does what I think is the wrong thing by me, I walk away and forgive them straight away then carry on with my own life. Life is too short to carry negativity and the burden that goes with it. It is times like these that you realise that some people are just not in the same space as you. Let it go and travel light.

I can honestly say that this particular vision and experience with my father was one of the most valuable and humbling experiences of my life. It has left a large impression with me and in reality, I acknowledge that I am one of the lucky ones as I was able to make peace with my father even after he had passed on. I will always be grateful for this and as a result, have always made sure I forgive people even after they have done wrong by me. I do not need to tell them; I just forgive and move on.

Leanne continued to go and see Chanty the psychic whenever she visited Kalgoorlie to run readings. She began to get quite an insight into her own past and present as I had now started to see Chanty also in regard to my own situation.

Not long after the experience with my father, I had a friend of mine die from injuries sustained in a mining accident. I was shell shocked as he was a great guy who had two sons and an awesome wife. Leanne and I had been friends with them for many years and his family were like our second family. They were a pakeha family originally from Te Aroha in New Zealand but had been in Australia for a very long time and now called WA home.

It had been a very sad time for everyone who knew Clifford, he was taken so young from us. His young family were devastated as were his brothers, sister and parents.

I actually got a bit depressed because just weeks after Cliffs death, we had a presentation by a mine workers widow at work on a presentation and book she had written addressing mining deaths in Western Australia from 1986 to 1993. The book was called Just A Number. If you manage to find a copy, have a read. It will give you a good wake up call.

During this time there were a total of seventeen people killed in mining accidents in Western Australia. Not the whole of Australia, just Western Australia. Out of the people who were named in the statistical records presented, I personally knew fifteen of these people including the latest name on the list, which of course was Clifford.

Chanty happened to be in town, and I was feeling a bit down in light of the recent events and I decided to go and see her.

As what was becoming habit when I walked in the door, she held it open for my 'entourage' as we came to call the entity's she saw walking behind me.

I told her I was actually specifically looking for someone called Clifford and she said she would try her best, but it was up to them if they wanted to come across.

Anyway, she started channelling and started passing messages to me saying how he was ok but the language she was using was so prim and proper, I told her, 'nah…. that's not him.'

She started talking quietly and said she could not do that, and her voice started getting louder.

She finally looked back to me and said, he has asked me to repeat a message for you word for word. He said you will not believe it's him if I change the words.

She went on to say she would not normally speak like this, but she had agreed to do it as he was very persistent that I would not believe it was him. Yeah, no worries, I replied.

With that, she re channelled Clifford and came out with the following, word for word.

'Ron, it's me mate, how the f*** are ya, it's me f*** ya'.
I looked at Chanty and said, 'yeah that is the Clifford I know'.

He was a hard case rogue bloke, scrawny in stature but who swore like a trooper and was funny as. He didn't have to try to be funny, just his mannerisms, expressions and language used to leave everyone in stitches. On occasions I saw Cliff and his brother Rob having an argument and they would both have veins popping out of their heads with faces flushed and I would just crack up laughing at them as they looked funny as. They would both stop and look at me and as my laugh is loud and booming, they would just crack up laughing at my laugh. I have had many great laughs with these guys. I never met another couple of blokes who would make my sides ache from laughing so hard.

Anyway, once I was satisfied it was indeed Cliff, Chanty carried on with the reading asking me to pass a message on to his widow and two sons telling her that he loved them, and he was in a good place. I did actually pass that message on a few days later. He then went on to describe a bit about where he was and how great it was, although he regretted leaving his family.

What really got me emotional was when she went on to describe a conversation, I had had with Cliff a few months earlier in the

Denver City Hotel in Coolgardie. I was on days off and Cliff was working at Tindall's mine, the mine where he eventually lost his life.

I had gone to the pub for a couple of brews and Cliff had stopped in for a beer before heading home to Kalgoorlie.

Chanty relayed the conversation from Clifford that we had that night and I knew no one could know what we spoke about. It was just two mates having a beer and discussing family life and such. It was a pretty deep conversation we had that night, pretty impressive considering we were both miners. Mind you we were also drunk.

Anyway, as I said, Chanty relayed this conversation and at the end of it she said Cliff was a bit sad that he no longer had that part of his life with him. I actually felt a bit sad for him as well. He had a beautiful wife Tasha and the boys Cliff junior and Robbie were awesome kids. He then told Chanty that if he had to live his life over again, he would not change it. It was an experience that had taught him many things and led to him meeting many awesome people and for that reason he could not change it even if he wanted to. The only regret he had was leaving his family.

This part of the reading ended with Cliff asking me to be sure to pass on his message, which as I said, I did a few days later when time permitted, and then telling me he had so much more to explore where he was. In hindsight, I can now look back at this and many other situations, not only with mediums but also of my own personal experience, where I have been allowed to experience conversations or even experiencing things as if I was there, with spirit who have passed over. I now know that I was actually being guided by Atama in order that I could learn not only from the experience but also learn how to get there on my own, from the dimension I currently exist in.

Chanty then continued with something she had told me many months previously. You know that you are being protected and guided don't you, to which I replied that she had told me previously.

I just mentioned it again because the chief behind you has asked me to remind you, she said.

She went on to tell me that his energy was the strongest of any she had ever seen and that his energy was as strong now as it was when he was among the living. She proceeded to tell me that he said that I need to find someone to help me, to tutor and mentor me as I needed to learn many things. Just trust that when the time is right, that person will be there for you she told me. She then went on to tell me that there were many behind this chief and she believed one of them was my father. I explained to her the experience I had a few days earlier and she said he will be here whenever I need him, he will be here to help me.

The reading finished with me feeling good knowing that Clifford was ok but slightly bemused at the thought of being told I was to learn many things. All I could think of was, what things but now I was glad dad was still here to help me.

I hugged Chanty and left. As I walked out, she told me to slow down, my entourage was saying I walk too fast.

I drove home with a lot of questions going through my head, none of which I had the answer for. What was I to learn? Who was going to teach me? What field were these lessons to be in? These questions were a lot closer to being answered than I had known at the time.

Chanty was in town for the next week and Leanne had a booking with her on her last day in town.

It was one or two months after I had that reading, we got a phone call from home telling me that my Uncle Tom Walsh had passed away.

Uncle Tom was a kind-hearted and gentle man. I remember many times that I had sat and spoken with him. I felt I could have told him anything, he just had that effect on me. He made me feel safe. I remember thinking to myself if only I had known him in my younger years. He kept a portrait of Atama Paparangi on his wall as I do and would speak to the portrait as if Atama was present in the room. Some of the things he told me in our conversations strongly indicated a very spiritual nature. He was a very humble man and that made me feel very much at ease. When we were living in New Zealand we would on occasion, Leanne, Brett and I, stop in to Baileys Beach on our way home from the farm and stay the night with Uncle Tom and Aunty Alice and even though I did not realise it at the time, he was giving me an insight into spirituality which would come to serve me in later years. I had enjoyed the times I had spent with him, even though those times were too few.

The end of the week arrived, and Leanne went to her reading with Chanty. When she got home, she was blown away with what she had been told.

She said the reading started as normal but then Chanty was relaying what she was seeing. The chief that normally follows me was in full ceremonial dress and there was a ceremony being conducted. She described the warriors and the dancing (like a haka she had told Leanne) and then she asked if someone in our family had recently passed. Leanne told her about Uncle Tom passing away. Chanty described to Leanne this other person that was being welcomed, and she recognised the description as being Uncle Tom. He was being welcomed home to this other dimension by Atama. Atama had described himself as the keeper in an earlier reading and when I had casually mentioned it to my mother, she had said the keeper of the clan. With what Leanne was telling me, I was beginning to see what this role of keeper actually was.

We sat there talking about it and then Leanne told me that she also had been given a message. It was to let Aunty Alice know that Uncle Tom was happy and in a good place and not to worry about him.

We rang her in New Zealand the next day and passed on the

message. She was glad to hear it and seemed to put her at ease after her loss.

It would have been no fewer than a few days after this that Brett started being affected again by things spiritual. For some reason I just knew it had nothing to do with anything from home.

I rang Chanty in Perth and had a chat with her. I told her that I did not know what was going on, but I knew it was not from home. Leanne and I had already talked about things and I asked Chanty if she would come and live with us for a week and could use Leanne's shop to do readings. I just wanted her to be with us and try to ascertain what was going on. Brett was seeing a man walking around the house and was being woken and teased by this entity.

Anyway, Chanty agreed and arrived the following week. Leanne had made up flyers and passed the word around in her salon that Chanty would be in town for the week and the bookings began rolling in.

Within the first day, Chanty had seen the spirit that was causing the disturbance and asked about the area. I told her what I could, and she asked me to do a bit of research on the land our house was on.

Brett took an instant liking to Chanty and in the afternoons him and Georgie his dog would take her for walks around town and over to the Pioneer Cemetery. She had taken a look at some of the headstones which dated back to the 1700s and asked about them.

I didn't really know much about them but apparently back in the gold rush days Coolgardie was a city with only Fremantle being the larger city in the state. Because of the poor conditions at the time a plague swept the area and many people died as a result. Chanty said that she could still feel many of these souls still around the area.

As she had asked, when I was on my days off, I went to the local museum and did some research on the block of land we were on. I discovered that back in the day a hotel stood on the block where our house now stood. There were 85 pubs and three breweries in town back in the goldrush. The story behind many of the pubs in the area was that murders had taken place on many occasions all over gold. I could not associate any of these stories with that particular pub or even settle on one name as it had been known by so many names.

Toward the end of the week, Chanty had told me that she had seen the spirit again and it seemed to be an old prospector. She had asked him what he wanted but he would not answer so she had asked him to leave and guided him to the light.

She told me that on many occasions she has witnessed a situation where someone has passed over, but they don't think they have. They linger and as there is no perception of time when you pass over, you could be there for years. It is at times like this she told me, you need to help them get to the light. I was shown this place as part of my training and it is referred to as limbo. Souls may be here until they realise, they have passed and find their way to the light.

These souls suffered a quick death and as such do not believe they have passed at all.

I have personally assisted in this capacity on a number of occasions since this instance. I must say, it can be difficult to comprehend it all and sometimes I do not know the circumstances of passing or have never even known the person in life. But what I have come to accept as true, is that the light is the destination we are all looking for after we leave this life. It was a piece of information which has helped me on many occasions.

The day Chanty was leaving, we were sitting under the patio having a cuppa when she suddenly asked if I knew what the cause of all of these instances had been. I looked at her and asked her if I was supposed to know. She sat in silence for a few minutes and then continued. Have you accepted that you have a role to play and that is why you are being protected and guided?

I told her that even though I had been told this on several occasions, I cannot see why it would be me. I told her that the role she has been describing to me as being my role in life does not seem real to me as I look at myself as just a normal person. A smile crossed her face as she looked at me and said, you are already a humble person, that is one of the hardest lessons to learn, yet you have already achieved this trait. There are several reasons you have been chosen Ron. You have a pure and good heart. You have already demonstrated that you are a humble person and finally, you have the determination to finish whatever you start. This will not be an easy road for you to travel but you have the abilities required to complete the journey. It is your journey to complete Ron. I didn't really say much, as I was mulling over what she had said. At that stage, I did not know how to accept positive feedback or compliments as they had been few and far between in my lifetime. Truth is I still have issues with it now.

She then continued, you do know that in spiritual terms, your son is wide open, and he has already been chosen as the next person in your family to receive this gift. You have told me of all he has been through as a child, but you have the power to stop it Ron. All you have to do is accept it. He was chosen when you turned your back on them and look at what he has had to endure she said. I sat in silence and after several minutes I said to her that I would think about it. Again, she told me to find someone to help me, as the physical distance between Perth and Coolgardie meant she would not be in a position to help. She told me to learn to listen to my body and put it out to the universe what I was seeking. THEN LISTEN and wait for the answer she said.

She left about mid-afternoon and Leanne and I sat down that night and had a good talk about it all. By the time we went to bed, I was no closer to arriving at a conclusion than I was in the beginning. All I knew was that I wanted to do something to help Brett live a normal life without this spiritual stuff continually affecting him as well as us.

I managed to put it all out of my mind for a few days after this, as I have learnt that your logical mind has a way of making you block out anything it cannot fathom or understand, and it takes a lot

151

of practice to stop this from happening.

CHAPTER 10

Time to Step Up to The Plate

It was only a few days later that something happened which changed the whole situation. At this time, I must say that the actions I took which changed my whole perception of the situation were at best reckless and pretty damn stupid. I would not recommend the method I used to anyone else but in saying that, I did achieve my objective which was to establish a rock-solid foundation in trust, faith and understanding in regard to the instances which had affected my son and I over a long period of time. This is a first-hand account of the circumstances and will give you an insight into how far I was prepared to go to protect my son and to address the whole spiritual journey that had followed me since I was 7 years old.

I was working underground in a gold mine at the time as a line of sight remote bogger operator (remote bogging is the remote operation of a loader in the removal of gold bearing ore from a mining stope). I will not say for which company but those of you who knew me at the time will know. We were using cascade stoping methods at this particular mine which means working three levels at a time with the bulk of the dirt ending up on the bottom level.

Anyway, my machine had broken down and I was in the workshop when one of the truck drivers called over the radio that a light vehicle was needed at a certain level by another bogger operator. I was still going to be down for a while, so I grabbed a light vehicle and headed down to the level called for.

I got there and another remote operator was there who needed a light vehicle to get up to the toilets as the underground toilets were not working. I gave him the Ute and told him I would keep remote operations going for him to keep his tonnes up, he was stoked.

Line of sight remote operating requires that you can drive the machine for normal operations but when the machine was required to go into a stope, you got out of the machine and strapped a remote control box around your waist or hung it from a bracket over your shoulders. There would be a remote cuddy that would have been blasted out of the wall. This would be your safe place if the machine ran away in remote control mode.

Remote control loaders were introduced so that the physical loss of human life was minimised in this particular type of mining operation, due to the operator not being in the operator's cabin if there was a cave in and the machine was buried. It proved to be a very safe practice for inside the stope. The industry then had a spate of operators running themselves over or squashing themselves against the walls with the machines in remote control causing the industry to look for other options to implement. Tele remotes were finally introduced to overcome the problems of deaths while remoting. The safety record for this function of mining has vastly improved. Tele remoting requires the operator to still remotely operate the machine but from out of the operational area and from a tele hut using TV screens and cameras. It is a much safer practise.

Anyway, I was doing line of sight remoting and picking up the pace when all of a sudden, these thoughts of how I was being protected came back into my head out of nowhere.

I was not trying to think about it at all, it was just there and try as I might, I just could not get it out of my head. What I did next still shocks me even to this day. I was driving the loader back to the cuddy from the stockpile when I suddenly stopped, looked up at the backs (roof of the tunnel) and said, 'well if you really are protecting me, prove it'.

I engaged the transmission and drove into the stope. I filled the bucket, went out to the stockpile and tipped and then headed back to the stope. This went on for two buckets but when I approached the brow on the third run, I heard a voice. I never hear it through my ears, I heard it in my mind, in my thoughts and it said one word only. Stop.

I immediately stopped the machine about 5 metres back from the brow and watched listening to the ground. First there was a trickle of small rocks coming down inside the stope and all of a sudden, all hell broke loose and tonnes of dirt came crashing down out in front of me. I threw the machine into reverse and floored it. Thick dust was coming out of the stope and the percussion of the fall pushed it out faster than the machine could move. I could not see the walls anymore, just thick dust, so I stopped the machine and made

155

sure my dust mask was sealed properly.

I was there for quite a few minutes when I saw a haze of light coming up behind me. It was the Ute headlights entering the level. The other operator was returning. When the dust had cleared, I got out of the cab and my mate came running up from the Ute. Dust was falling off of me as I exited the cab. It was an open cab, so it didn't have any windows. The loaders were all like this back in the day.

When the dust had settled, we walked up around the corner to the stope and it was choked off. There must have been at least a few thousand tonnes of dirt come down and if I had been out there in the loader, I would have been history for sure.

My mate was going on about how lucky I was that I wasn't remoting from the brow as I had told him I was coming back from the stockpile when it fell in. He assumed that where he saw the loader when the dust cleared was where I had stopped it when the fall in happened. I never told him any different.

For the first time, I actually felt and accepted that I was being protected and guided. The voice in my head, the whole situation, just confirmed to me that I was indeed being protected. Knowing this, I now felt that I had to discover why I was being protected, what it was that I needed to do. What am I here for?

I got home the following morning and Brett had gone off to school and Leanne was just having a coffee before she opened the shop for the day. I grabbed a coffee too and told her what had happened. Man did she hit the roof and in reality, I don't blame her. To think back about it now even I think it was extreme and even reckless but as I said to her, I needed an answer, an answer that I could never question again, and I got what I asked for as far as I was concerned. "What if you had been killed" she screamed at me. I could not really answer that, I had never even considered that option. The only thing I did know was that I knew I was asking for something big, so I had to be prepared to lose something big in return. It was only at this point the full ramification of what I had done really hit home. I had put my life on the line in order to get an answer to a question, a question I felt needed to be answered and because the answer was so powerful, I have never felt the need to question anything I have been told during the course of my journey to this day. For once, I actually placed my trust into what I was being shown and told. I remember several months later saying to Leanne I now know what it is like to have faith in something.

It took a few days to settle things at home after this one. I have never done anything like that again and never will but at the time I needed an answer or, in fact, proof of what was being told to me. I can honestly say it was a game changer in my journey.

I tried to keep busy after this while things cooled down with Leanne and read through a prospectus, I had bought back from New Zealand given to me by Leonie and Ron, Leanne's parents.

I read about the operational benefits of this system which took large amounts of garbage and turned them into reusable products such as electricity, water and building materials.

I wrote a letter to their head office in Auckland and said that the parameters they needed to operate such a facility actually existed in Perth. The environmentalist in me came from out of nowhere and I sent the letter off not expecting to hear anything back.

It was not even a week later, and I had a reply to my letter from the Managing Director asking if I could call or supply a phone number so they could call me. I rang the number supplied and advised who I was, and the Managing Director and another Director immediately went on conference call. They asked how I came to be in possession of the information, and I explained how I received their prospectus.

They decided to come to Perth for a look and asked if I would be available to meet with them while they were over. We met a few weeks later in Perth together with another contact they had made in Perth through one of their investors.

We were in Perth for a week and by the time I was heading home, I had been appointed Project Manager for the Western Australian arm of the company. I had never had any experience in this area at all, so I was a bit apprehensive about it all and I was still working underground in the gold mining industry at the same time.

I was working four days on and four days off underground at this time, so on my days off I would fly to Perth to represent the project and conduct meetings in order to get things off the ground. I did not know it at the time, but it was going to be my training ground to hone some of the newfound skills I was to achieve during my upcoming training.

Brett was not having any more visitors and I was really giving some thought to what Chanty had told me about finding some help to mentor and guide me to what I needed to know.

After what happened in New Zealand and now what was going on here, I decided I needed to do something to allow Brett to have a normal childhood and not be tormented by all of the strange goings on he had so far experienced in his life. I told Leanne that I thought it was time I looked at what Chanty had said and decided I needed to see what it was all about and try to find a mentor or a teacher. She was a bit taken aback as this was the first time, I had actually decided to face these problems head on as it were.

Up to this point I found it had been extremely difficult to deal with something that you cannot see and touch but against everything I had ever been told as a young man I figured it was time to take the leap and try to deal with it rather than have it affect Brett for the rest of his life. Leanne and I both looked back on all we had endured in both countries and I said to her that the experience I had at work actually gave me a better feeling of what I was being told I needed to do. It also gave me a better understanding of my gift. I had been practicing listening to my body and putting things out to the universe and waiting for an answer. I told her I would use these same tactics to see how I proceeded from here. I don't know if she was happy with what I had decided but she offered her support if I needed it.

CHAPTER 11

Finding My Mentor and Finding My Feet

I did not know how to meditate at this stage, so all I did was to sit quietly. It took me a while to master quietening my thoughts and counting my breaths but the practice, I had already done had been quite effective even if I did not exactly know what I was doing. I put out to the universe that I was ready to accept my gift and would like someone to show me how to use it in a good way. I did this for two nights and then left it and waited for an answer.

The answer I received back arrived within a week. There was to be a Psychic Expo to be held at the Kalgoorlie Arts Centre with many mediums, clairvoyants and psychics available for readings or spiritual guidance. It was to take place the following week and I would be off work and could go. I told Leanne about it and told her I would go there and see what it had to offer and if I could find someone to mentor or teach me.

I could not tell her how I was going to do it, just that this was the plan. She just said to me, 'Oh well, good luck with it then'. I honestly did not know what I was looking for or how I was going to find what I was looking for, but I thought to myself, well it is a step in the right direction. It's a bit hard to explain what I was feeling then. I felt it was time to take the first step but at the same time, I did not know in which direction I should take that first step. From where I stood though, it seemed now that the decision had been made, any step would be better than nothing. That night I cleared my mind and put out to the universe that if this was indeed the direction I was supposed to be headed in, some help with getting started would be much appreciated.

It did not take long for the Psychic Expo to roll around. On that morning I had breakfast with the family, ran Brett to school and went home again to have a coffee with Leanne before heading into Kalgoorlie. I told her I felt a bit apprehensive, but I was sure this was the way forward. I was heading into new territory that up until now I had avoided like the plague. I was used to running from it, not embracing or accepting it. This new attitude was completely foreign to me, yet I just knew the time was right to do this.

I arrived at the expo and just walked around outside for a while having a cigarette and, in my mind, asking for guidance to find what I was seeking. I was enjoying walking around in the warm sunshine. It seemed to relax me and gave me a really good feeling.

I walked into the expo not knowing what I was looking for or what to expect. I asked my body to show me what or who I was looking for and just walked around browsing. There were stands for purchasing anything spiritual from crystals to meditation music and it did not feel uncomfortable at all, in fact it felt quite the opposite. I felt very comfortable in this setting. I wandered around all the exhibits and found the area where the readings were to be conducted and asked a woman how it all worked. She told me that there were a number of mediums who would be in and out over the next few days to conduct readings as required. All you had to do was find the one you liked, sit down and they would do a reading for you. Again, I asked my body for a signal and walked around the tables to see what would happen. Just as I thought, nothing. I never felt anything to give me an indication. I asked when the next change of readers would take place and was told at 1.00pm. It was only 11am at this stage so I decided to go and do some shopping while I waited. I thought I may as well try again with new readers while I was in town.

I did not get back to the expo till around 2pm. The new readers would be on till 4pm so I did not have any worries. Again, I asked my body to give me a signal as I went in. I approached the reading tables and again walked past them. As I did, I noticed my body had a warm feeling for an instant as I passed a certain medium. I continued to the end of the tables and nothing else. I retraced my steps and I got a warm feeling again when I passed that one particular medium. I checked it a few more times and sure enough, always at the same table I felt a warm sensation run through my body. My body was actually signalling me. This was a whole new thing for me and, to be honest, I was very excited. I went outside again and had a cigarette while I ran through my mind what had just happened.

I went over everything step by step and decided that yes, my body had just given me a signal, or an indication even. I thought to myself, is this the person that I am looking for? Could it really be this easy to get in touch with yourself? Still excited, I decided to go back in and try it again as soon as I had finished my cigarette.

I headed straight for the reading area. Again, I felt a warm sensation as I walked past this particular medium sitting at the same table as before. I walked away from the area and for the first time, I looked up at who was sitting at the table.

She was an attractive blonde woman who looked to be around my age. I stood there pondering how I was going to approach this and, in the end, just decided to walk up and see what would happen.

She was not doing a reading at the time, so I just casually walked up and sat down at her table. I introduced myself and she told me her name was Darleena. We started some small talk and she told me she had moved to Kalgoorlie a few months earlier and had just started doing readings again after settling in.

She proceeded to ask me if I wanted a reading, but I said no. I was just after some information. I went on to tell her a brief version of past events and how I came to be at the expo and the feeling of warmth every time I passed her table. She said, wow, and how can I help you. I took a deep breath and said, well, I was hoping you would be able to mentor or teach me. That is what I am here for today, to find someone to help me.

I sat there staring straight into her eyes when the saying 'the eyes are the windows to a person's soul' popped into my mind. I saw peace and knowledge in those eyes and then I noticed her eyes moving all around me before she finally spoke. I cannot help you sorry, she said still looking all around me. Ok can I ask why not I replied. After pausing for what seemed like a few minutes, she replied, I can see these men behind you, they are very powerful entities with very, very, strong energies. She then went on to describe what she called a man with tattoos all over his face and described the cloak of feathers of what I knew as customary Maori dress for that time. I cannot teach you what they can teach you, they are way above where I am at.

I sat there in silence and then without even thinking about it said to her, I do not want you to teach me what they know. I want you to teach me how to protect myself and anything important that you think I need to know, and I will take it from there.

Once again, she outright refused to help me saying that these entity's, she could see had energies so strong, she had never seen anything like it. She said she would be out of her depth in their company. I was disappointed but had to accept and respect her answer. I told her that if she changed her mind, could she please call me and handed her my business card. I then left and headed home and thought to myself try again tomorrow.

I got home and told Leanne what had happened. We were both disappointed, but I said I would go back tomorrow and see if they had any new readers there. The next day I went back to the expo and felt absolutely nothing. The woman I had met the previous day was not on that day. I had spent the whole day trying to find someone else, but the body gave me no signal whatsoever. I went home that day very disappointed in the fact that I had not found anyone that could or would help me. I knew that feeling only too well from my younger years.

Nothing at all happened for the next week but at the end of the following week things took a huge turn around. I had just flown back in from Perth working on the project and going through the airport when my mobile rang. I answered the phone and it was Darleena. She asked me if I had any luck finding a mentor or teacher, to which I replied I had no luck at all.

Again, she asked me exactly what I was looking for and again I told her someone to teach me how to protect myself and anything else I needed to know. I would take it from there I told her. There was a long silence on the phone before she answered, ok then, yes, I will help you. I jumped around outside the airport completely stoked. Anyone would have thought I had won lotto.

I thanked her and she reminded me, just remember, I can't teach you what they can teach you. That is fine I told her. We agreed to meet up and discuss everything on my next break in 4 days' time, so I headed for home. I had an overpowering feeling of happiness wash over me on the way home. This was going to be the beginning of, I didn't know what. I just knew it was the beginning of something and I felt it would be something big.

The following 4 days just flew past and, to be honest, I was not really thinking about what was going to happen. I just felt like nothing was a problem. The day that I was going into town to meet with Darleena I felt apprehensive but at the same time excited. I had arranged not to go to Perth this break as Ian in the Perth office would take care of things for me. I had a few small niggling doubts about it all, but they would never last for more than a few seconds before they vanished from my mind again. I took it as a sign that I was on the right track. For the first time in my life I was actually looking forward to facing up to my spiritual heritage rather than running from it and although it was foreign to me, the emotion I was experiencing through this period was nothing short of pure excitement. Again, I took this as a sign I was on the right track.

I arrived at Darleena's house around 1pm and what surprised me, as had happened with Chanty, was that she held the door open after I had entered, for my entourage. We just had a casual conversation so she could gauge where I was spiritually, I suppose. I now use this same technique to assess possible students for mentoring. We discussed all the past happenings even back as far as when I was a child. She was taking a few notes as we were speaking. I then noticed that she was looking around me again. She was silent for a while before she finally spoke to me. There are three men here with you. One of them calls himself the keeper and has tattoos all over his face. I told her I knew who he was and the series of events that had happened with Chanty. I went on to explain how Chanty had said I needed to find someone to help me as a teacher or mentor hence the reason I was here. She went on to describe the other two and I guessed one was my father, which she confirmed and the third was Uncle Tom Walsh, which she also confirmed.

She said they had told her they were here to help me also, but they could only stay for three months. They would assist with what I needed to learn with the help of Darleena in order that the lessons were conducted as practically and efficiently as possible.

We would begin the lessons the following day as she said she would need to do some preparation of her own, but she also wanted me to buy a coloured candle. I was to ask my body what colour it needed then to choose a candle with that colour.

Darleena instructed me to go home and prepare a room for myself that no one else was to enter for the duration of my training. This requirement was necessary in order to allow me to condense my own energy in one area to allow me to be able to reconnect with it as quickly as possible when needed, rather like putting your energy into an innate object as I explained earlier. The only difference was I would be putting my energy into a space and everything within that space.

I left her house and went straight to The Crystal Den, which was a shop in Kalgoorlie that sold crystals, books on meditation as well as CDs and of course candles. I went to the area where they displayed the candles and incense and such. I asked my body which colour it needed then closed my eyes. All of a sudden, my mind was filled with the colour blue, so I opened my eyes and walked to where the blue candles were. I held my hand out palm open and, facing the shelves, passed my hand over the blue candles. I felt a small tingle of energy in the palm of my hand when I passed over one particular blue candle. That was the one I picked up and purchased.

I headed home with my purchase and on the way, I stopped off and picked Brett up from school. He was happy to see me and proceeded to tell me all about his school day as I drove home.

That night when Leanne closed the salon we sat down for dinner. I explained to Leanne and Brett that I needed to set one room aside for me to use as a training room as Darleena had informed me and that I would be setting it up after dinner as the training would be starting the following day. We discussed any doubts and fears we had but as I said to Leanne, this has gone on long enough and I needed to face up to it. With that she supported the decision I had made. I figured that I wanted Brett to have as normal a childhood as possible because I never got that and that if I undertook my role, then when it was time for Brett to learn I could help him. He would have someone to turn to, unlike my situation where I had no one to turn to.

Brett was present during most of our discussions and began picking up on things we were talking about. In fact, he began to close off a bit and started to always want to know what was happening with me. On one night in particular, it was a time the moon was closer to the earth than it had ever been, Brett asked me to show him how to meditate. We had this large futon cane lounge under the back patio so after dinner we dragged it out into the centre of the back lawn, lay the top flat and both got comfortable. I walked him through a guided meditation using the massive moon above us as subject matter. I then asked him to open his eyes and refocus. After a few minutes I asked him to explain to me what he saw. He could see a bright white light stairway coming down from the moon but the end of it was waving around in the sky as it was coming down to earth. He kept telling me how it was shifting and changing as it moved through the night sky and it was falling to earth. He kept talking and then he started getting excited saying dad, dad, it's going to land here. Finally, he was so excited the end of the stairway landed in our backyard and then, as we watched, it went from being a floppy stairway to what you would think was a rigid structure. We sat there and he was amazed at what he saw. I just told him to watch it for a while before I told him to send it back to the moon. I got a running commentary from him explaining how it was going back up into the sky when he suddenly said it's all gone dad. We sat out there for a few minutes just watching the moon. Brett asked me if he did well. I just said, yes son you did well. What I did not tell him was that he was seeing the exact same images I was seeing. It was the meditation I had created just for him with every detail bringing excitement and a huge smile to his face. He was wide open and on his first meditation he got there he had got to the place he was meant to. I did not tell him that at the time as I was getting a bit worried at how involved he was getting with what was going on around him. If you are reading this book Brett, dad is so proud of you. You got there buddy, I was so proud of you, but I never told you at the time because I wanted you to have the carefree childhood I never had. I made a mental note to myself to keep a close eye on him.

When we went back inside the house, I decided to make a start on preparing a training room for myself now that my lessons were to start. I chose the smallest room to use and started moving things out and into another spare room. I did not know what I was preparing for, so I took a guess and left a single bed, a small coffee table and an armchair in the room and removed everything else. I placed a CD player in the room too, just in case.

I could see Brett was trying to keep up with me, so I took him aside and sat him down for a talk. I told him that I wanted him to step back from all of this spiritual stuff and enjoy his childhood and his mates. You are far too young to take this on your shoulders Brett so I want you to walk away from it and dad will take care of it so that when you are ready to look into all of this, I will be there to help and guide you rather than have you flounder as I have had to do. I told him I loved him and gave him a big hug. All he said to me was, OK dad. He did walk away from it and it was good to see him enjoy his childhood.

The rest of the evening went off without a hitch. Brett had a bath and we put him to bed and then as we normally did, Leanne and I would have a cup of coffee and just talk. She was still a bit apprehensive about me doing what I was going to do but I told her it had to be done. I told her about the conversation I had with Brett earlier and she told me she also noticed he was getting too involved in it, so she was glad I told him to step away from it.

I had decided that since it had followed me all my life it was time to step up to the plate. I had surprised even myself since the fear had now gone and I was now ready to learn about what had been with me for so long. In fact, I was put at ease as both Chanty and Darleena could see Atama, my dad and my uncle. It just seemed to make things ok with me I suppose.

The following day began with the same routine. I was still on my days off, so I ran Brett to school and then came home to do some work on the Perth project I was working on as Project Manager. I had Ian on the ground in Perth so I would plan what needed to be done and get him to set up meetings and phone conferences for me. At the time it did not require me to be in Perth every break as it was in its infancy stage, so much of the work I was doing could be done from home.

I had told Leanne the night before that my appointment was for 1pm so she had intentionally kept her schedule free from 11.30am to 12.30pm. I stopped working when she came into the house and we made up a quick lunch and had a cuppa. She wished me good luck and I headed off in time to get to Kalgoorlie by 1.00pm.

I was still walking up the path to the front door when Darleena opened the door for me. I remember the dress she was wearing, a white mid-thigh skirt with a floral arrangement print on it. I remember thinking to myself WOW. She had just got home herself as I arrived.

Anyway, as was getting to be the norm, she held the door open after I walked through for my entourage and we went into her lounge room. She had set up a small glass top table with two seats. She motioned for me to take a seat, which I did. After she closed the door, she took a seat on the opposite side of the table. I must admit, I did notice her legs through the glass top table, they looked awesome. After all, I am only human and not a saint by a long shot.

We spoke of what we would be hoping to achieve in general

terms and then Darleena went all quiet. I looked at her and she was looking around me. After a while she hadn't said anything, so I just said, 'what?' She remained silent for a few more minutes before again speaking with me. We have a situation here Ron she said. There are now two very powerful chief energies here both wanting to teach you. Do you know who the other is she asked. I explained to her how our family is the result of two Rangatira (chief) bloodlines being joined through marriage of my mother and father. She told me they were indicating that what I said was true. I explained that they were both Rangatira (Chief) and Tohunga (Healer) to which she told me they were nodding their heads in agreement. She was silent for a few seconds looking all around me and then even from one side of the room to another. She told me I was going to have to make a choice. You cannot take both Chiefs, she told me. You have to make a choice which one you will follow she said. I thought for a second then looked at her and said, Atama my great great great grandfather and Rangatira from Mitimiti, I will follow him. She went on to tell me that the other rangatira, my great great grandfather on my mothers' side, Anaru, told her that he does not want to be left behind and forgotten so he will choose another. She then told me that because I was given the choice, I would also be able to see who Anaru had chosen when he had decided, as that person would not be given a choice. She then went silent again for a minute or so then came back and said that Anaru had left the room.

Darleena and I went on to discuss how the training would proceed and she also told me she had prepared herself for this lesson the night before.

She had been shown where to lead me in the training and she was comfortable with it but then added, to be honest, most people would take years to come to terms with what I need to show you. I reminded her that I was told I had three months to learn to which she replied, yes, I know they believe you can do it in the timeframe. I just looked at her and said, oh well, we better get started then and after a few seconds silence she just started laughing and said Atama had just told her, he has awoken now that is why he is here. He will make sure he completes what he needs to, he is that determined.

She told me that the entire course was going to be meditation based as this would be the best and most effective method to teach me. She asked if I had meditated before to which I replied I had not really been shown but have tried some on my own or used guided meditations. She explained that it was a method used to shut out the everyday noise of the life we are living while also allowing us to close down any thoughts or doubts in our minds. To work with a blank canvas was the term she used. She explained that she had taught meditation on a regular basis while she was in Perth and it was actually up to the individual on how fast or how slow they were to proceed and it was usually based on how far their journey had already progressed and what they had learnt from it so far. This gave me an interesting insight into why we were here, and we all have something to complete while we are here on this plane. She also went on to explain the importance of so-called coincidences and how they are not really coincidences but signposts or clues for your inner self to pick up on.

From where I stand today, I can now see the value of this statement and with the benefit of hindsight, I am now able to look back and see, yes, they were signposts and they not only contributed to but defined the direction of the path I was to take from that point on. It is really amazing to look back on all these coincidences and see how they fit into the big picture. They are actually like locking stones that lock all of these fragments of thought together which then forms a crystal-clear picture. It is at this point you then see how everything fits together and the importance of these so-called coincidences. The overview that she was giving me was actually setting me up in a way that during my classes and even the sessions I had on my own, when certain questions were raised, this information she had given me automatically gave me an answer. When I realised that I did actually know how it all worked, I was not only astonished, but I also had a warm feeling inside that told me that yes, I have awoken. I also realised that all of the scenarios that were being explained to me were not foreign to me but rather unleashed thoughts and visions which told me I already knew this stuff and, somehow, it was the right fit, like a glove.

She went on to explain that I should not be upset if nothing happens today, it just takes practice and that today's lesson would involve learning how to focus all of my thoughts and energies into a single object or point of vision.

By focussing, she continued, you will learn to focus intently in order that you can shut down your daily life as well as that little voice in your head that we call logic as quickly as possible. She explained to me that this little voice in your head known as logic has been bred into us due to the changes in the world and the environment around us. It will try to stop us from embracing spirituality as it will no longer be able to control us once we reconnect with our higher selves.

Back when we, as a race of people, were more spiritual beings, the important things in life were peace, love, harmony, balance and an amazing sense of well-being. With the so-called progression of our species it seems the important things in life are now dependant on one thing. Money. I must admit, I had never even thought about this before but as she spoke, I had a mental picture in my mind showing me in pictures, like a loop video, what she was explaining to me. I thought to myself, wow, this is unreal. The fact that this happened actually allowed me to see an in-depth view of what she was explaining, and it really did put things in perspective for me on a spiritual level, which up until now was foreign to me. It was at this point that I came to the realisation that I was actually being shown something that was so complex on so many levels while at the same time it was very easy for me to digest. Sounds a bit contradictory I know but it is what it is.

Before we started, she stressed to me again, do not be disappointed if you do not get it straight away. Many people take years to master this one lesson as it can be very difficult for someone to disengage from their everyday life even for a short period of time.

But that is the secret to learning this way, she said.

She lit the candle and started some soothing meditation music and asked me to close my eyes while we prepared ourselves for the session ahead. She walked me through the process acknowledging thoughts and then letting them go temporarily until I had done what I needed to do. This is how I trick logic so that my mind would become quiet and calm. We acknowledge what logic says to us but then acknowledge and put it to the side while we do what we need to do.

We then went on and she asked me to picture someone who had passed on that I knew. In my minds' eye, I saw Atama in my thoughts. I had never met him in person, but I recognised his face by paintings I had seen at home and also in the Auckland Museum. She told me that this person was there to protect my door, but I needed to ask them to take that role, which I did. It actually set my mind at ease as when I had a reading by Chanty, she had told me that he called himself the keeper, the keeper of the Clan she said. I felt safe in the knowledge that he was now my keeper, the keeper to my doorway to the other side. She then asked me to ask for my guide or guides to come forward. Again, in my mind's eye I saw three faces. These faces were Atama, my father and my great Uncle Tom Walsh.

I can still remember today how dad and Uncle Tom looked before they passed but now when I see them on the other side, they look younger and in their prime. My father and uncle now both have a moko on their face. I later learnt how that came to be during the course of my training. I find everyone I see on the other side is younger and in their prime, so I guess it is just how it is, and I accept that. If I do not recognise them, I ask them to reveal themselves to me, so I know who they are and then they age before me to who they were when I last saw them. At first, it kind of freaked me out but then I just thought to myself, well they are allowing me to see them as I know them, so I accepted it as a good thing.

Finally, she asked me to again focus and see what my nature sign was. She told me that my nature sign can be any living thing that is not human. It can be animal, bird insect, whatever. The significance of this part of the process was to acknowledge mother earth by choosing another one of her miraculous gifts as a protector and also the acknowledgement that every living thing on this planet is a living energy with a soul.

I focussed and after a very short time I saw an Eagle. What was really strange was, it was so real, like it was standing right in front of me. It moved around me, but its eyes never left mine, it just seemed to be examining me I suppose. It was a real surreal moment that I will never forget.

She told me that the Eagle may not specifically represent an Eagle. It may be a representation of birds in general, but the future will reveal the true meaning of the Eagle. In saying this, hindsight has again shown me that since this time, I have attracted birds in abundance in most places I go and especially where I live. I did tell my mother about this on one occasion and she told me that in Maoridom having birds always around you is a sign that you are being protected. When I was doing Fly in Fly out work in Perth, my neighbours said to me that they love it when I come home on break as all the birds would return. I was completely unaware they would leave when I flew out to work. In fact, I would have Willy Wagtails come right into the lounge to see me when I would leave the sliding door open and a Kookaburra would arrive at my house the first morning, I was home on every break. He would ram the fly screen on the kitchen window and hit the glass with his beak. I would stand there and speak to him, 'oi mate, I know you are here so stop ramming the glass and chill out.' Each time after I spoke with him, he would sit on top of the garage and watch me all day through the windows. He would crack me up. The Willy Wagtails were very inquisitive and at times would stand in the lounge for what seemed like hours just watching me while I played guitar. When not inside, the Willy Wagtails would join the many birds that would be all over my front lawn just watching through the front windows. It was awesome to observe. One year I went home with a friend and went up into the Warawara Forest. For the entire time I was in there, a Fantail bird escorted me all the way into the forest to the first hut and back out again. My friend asked what it meant, and I just said it was just checking to see who was coming into the forest and left it at that. The amazing thing about this experience was that the Fantail just kept hopping from branch to branch continually circling me all the way in as far as the tramping hut and then all the way out of the forest again. The other thing that we both noted was the absolute silence of the forest as we walked through it. You could not hear the sea or any other wildlife, just the sound of our steps and the flitter of the Fantail's wings. It was a very surreal experience.

After a time Darleena spoke again in a calming tone and I was told to thank the Eagle for all that had been revealed to me.

Darleena's calm smooth voice then instructed me to relax and slowly open my eyes when ready and focus on the flame of a candle on the tabletop. She told me that the purpose of this exercise was to teach me to control the flame of the candle with my mind. Once you have learnt to control that flame with your mind, you have demonstrated that you are able to fully focus on your objective, which means you will find it very easy to enter into a meditative state very quickly and without having conflict with logic for long periods. It was an exercise to free my mind to respond to my own thoughts and not to the voice of logic.

Just as I was getting into it, I noticed Darleena's legs through the table. It must be a man thing. Anyway, I re-focussed on what I was doing and almost immediately began to experience some amazing sensations and visions. The whole room changed colour and shape while every object in the room still had its relativity in this changing kaleidoscope of colour and form. It was at this time that I experienced one of the most amazing sensations of my mind moving through space, into another dimension.

As this lesson proceeded, Darleena would continue with the guided meditation and at times she would ask what I was experiencing and then move on again as soon as I had informed her. It put me at ease being able to hear her voice but feeling that I was in a completely different space to her. It felt like she was my safety line or training wheels to be more precise.

I found that I have the capacity to focus very quickly with the aid of guided meditation. The energy I was feeling was nothing short of euphoric and I felt as if I was just floating everywhere. I was able to carry out dictated exercises while achieving results almost immediately and I was both surprised and elated by that.

A couple of times her excitement at me getting immediate results broke my concentration and I would find my gaze back on her legs. Each time I managed to refocus and continue with the lesson. I had never felt such an awesome feeling of being free as I did on this first lesson. For some reason I had never thought of myself as being constrained until I felt what it was like to be free.

At the completion of the guided meditation we sat and discussed what I had experienced and what I had achieved. Darleena told me that I was more than ready for this journey as she had never seen anyone just walk in sit down and do what I did. She also mentioned that at times she sensed I was failing in focus. I was honest with her and told her when her voice got excited it would break my concentration and then my gaze would fall on her legs. She laughed at what I said and then I said, 'I would appreciate it if you could wear jeans or such from here on in. Your legs look awesome, but I only have limited time to learn this stuff you know'.

She apologised and we both laughed. From that day on, she wore jeans, or a long dress and we concentrated all our efforts on what I needed to learn. She is a beautiful soul and is a truly beautiful nurturing being.

She told me to keep practicing at home for the next week and work on a routine at the same time on each day. She explained that normally, she would leave it up to the student to dictate when they were ready for the next lesson but as we had limited time and I was getting such good results, we just set up the next appointment for the following week.

Well I went home that afternoon fully energised and full of excitement. I was to go back to work underground that evening so when I got home quickly checked that the room I had chosen as my meditation room was ready to start using the following morning.

That night I went to work and still felt a bit excited about starting my sessions the next morning. The results of my session with Darleena that day just kept playing through my mind over and over. The night flew by.

Well the following morning, I got home from work had a quick cup of coffee, went to say hi to Leanne in her salon when she got back from dropping Brett to school and then retired to the meditation room to practice. I darkened the room and put on some flute music and sat in the chair ready to begin. I remembered a timer Leanne had in the shop, so I lit the candle then raced out to get it. I set it for 25 mins then shut it outside the bedroom door and again settled into my chair to begin.

I began by releasing and letting go and almost immediately had the hairs on the back of my neck stand up. I was focussing on the candle when a face appeared behind the flame. It was Atama and the light of the flame danced across his face. Just the way it happened had caused a startled reaction from me as I was not expecting it. The way the candlelight was dancing across his facial moko and shadowing his eyes would be enough to make anyone jump. When I realised who it was, I had to settle myself down before I greeted him and then continued with my session.

He sat there intently watching offering silent encouragement to practise the lesson before me while every so often he would respond with a slight smile. From time to time he would give me a small nod of his head and his smile would become broader across his face. I took this as a sign that he was happy with the results I was achieving.

I continued to complete the exercises once again getting to the stage where I could exert some influence over the flame and control its movements by my thoughts. Like anything else that you learn, I found I was getting better at it and managing to put different thoughts together which would then result in the changes in movement of the flame. Even I was excited and happy with my progress.

When the timer alarm went off, I silently gave thanks, bid farewell to Atama and extinguished the flame.

I was happy with my session and being exhausted after working night shift, I retired to bed and slept the day away. I awoke late in the afternoon around 6pm and felt like a million bucks. I was so energised I swear I was ready to start pinging off the walls. I had dinner with Leanne and Brett and then headed off for work.

The following morning when I got home from work, I had a coffee with Leanne and again retired to the room to practice my sessions.

This morning, I turned on the music, set the alarm and then lit the candle. As I got up to switch off the lights, I glanced at the candle and Atama was already sitting behind the flame smiling at me and waiting. I quickly turned off the light and took my place in my armchair. Knowing that he was already there with me somehow made it so easy for me to transition from where I was to where I needed to be. Again, I noticed that this was getting easier and easier to control the flame, to focus intently on the flame. After all the whole exercise was about learning to focus on a single point or area. The discipline of the mind.

I continued to practice for the remainder of the week and even began making it physically harder for myself to maintain focus. For instance, our house had an evaporative ducted air-conditioning system throughout. I began turning it on during the week and increasing the velocity of air being delivered through the ducting each day. The idea was that by introducing a physical variable, which would be the airflow generated in the room, it would require more focus or effort on my part to control the flame of the candle. To be honest I did not really know if it would work but it tends to get boring doing the same thing day in and day out for me, so I tried it.

I always come up with stuff like this.

Well I must say that I even impressed myself. I noticed that each day after I increased the velocity, initially I could not control the flame but, by the end of the session, I had managed to overcome the physical variable I had introduced and regained control of the flame. I tell you what, it was a pretty exciting time for me. It might sound a bit boring to most people but managing to increase the intensity of your focus on a daily basis is a big thing and the huge smile on Atama's face told me that this is what he was wanting me to achieve.

At the end of the week, the day before I was due to go back to Darleena, I gave myself the biggest test so far. I turned the air-conditioning (AC) to full and went into the room to prepare myself. It took me a little while, but I managed to tame the flame. Even though I could physically feel the air rushing around the room from the outlet, I could feel energy rushing through me as I intensified my focus on the flame. The sensation was one which made me feel completely energised. As I said earlier, it makes you feel like you are going to start pinging off the walls. It took a while but again, I managed to maintain focus on the flame and by doing this I also gained control of the flame. Stand up, drop down, go wide and stand up straight among others were the commands I was sending to the flame and through my own eyes I saw the flame respond to my commands.

The sensation is something I have never experienced in any other situation in my life, so it was new to me but also very exciting and unbelievably empowering. In short, it was a real rush.

I finished up the session once the alarm had rung and once again gave thanks and bid farewell to Atama before rushing out to tell Leanne what had happened. She was almost as excited as I was. It was hard to explain exactly what had happened, what with all the excitement within me, as well as the fact that nothing like this had ever happened to me before. I had not experienced anything even remotely as powerful and empowering as I had just been subject too. It was just too awesome to fully comprehend but there were many days ahead where these experiences and emotions would return, it would just be in much larger doses.

I slept in the following morning as it was my first day off from work. I was not booked in to see Darleena until 1.00pm so I ran Brett to school, had a coffee with Leanne and thought I would go back to bed. Wrong. I found I could not get back to sleep and the events that happened the day before began playing through my mind again. After a small while, I just looked at the ceiling and said to no one, 'ok, I get it, you want me to go practice again'.

I got up and went and prepared myself for another session.

As normal, I turned on the music, lit the candle and saw Atama behind the candle flame as I turned off the lights. From here everything changed. The AC was actually off as it was a fairly cool day and it was Atama who suddenly began blowing the flame with his breath causing it to flicker and sway.

I sat down in my armchair and began to focus on the flame and then commanded it to stand still which it did. He then blew harder and I had to refocus and command the flame once again to stand still. Once again it stood still. Then he kept up a consistent blowing to make it even more difficult for me and I grabbed the arms on the chair and really intensified my focus on the flame. I felt a rush of energy go up my legs through my body, then down my arms and out to the flame through the tips of my fingers. The flame stood tall and straight while Atama continued to blow. After a while he stopped blowing the candle, gave me a big broad smile, gave me a nod of his head and turned away. He was gone. I had been tested and I had passed.

I went to my appointment with Darleena and thanked her for wearing jeans (it became a bit of a standing joke after day one and she had a bit of a laugh). I walked in while she held the door open for my entourage, as she also liked to call them. Once she had closed the door and come inside, we sat down and I described what had happened over the past week and in particular, this morning. She told me that she was amazed I had got that far in a week and while looking up behind me she said, 'your grandfather is very happy with your progress'. She then looked at me and told me that I was more than ready for my journey as I was picking it up so easily, but she said she was not surprised with the help of the three behind me. She informed me that most people can take months or even years to get through this first lesson as many find it hard to leave everything they have learnt and know, even for a short period of time, just to let go and be free.

From my perspective, I actually agreed with her. From being someone who had been bought up to fear spirituality to now embracing it and being absolutely blown away in a good way by what I was experiencing, I now actually felt alive, awake or whatever you want to call it, but I knew I felt good, even dynamic.

We moved onto the next session which was using colour to balance your energies and recharge your wairua (spirit). At the end of the session, I have got to say, I felt on top of the world. We discussed the session and what I got out of it and Darleena was again blown away that I picked it up again on the first try.

We sat and talked about the sessions and I had some questions I needed to ask her. I asked her how she knew what I needed to learn next. She said Atama told her and it was based on how I performed on the previous lesson. She went on to tell me that I was not yet able to communicate directly with my soul so Atama was acting as a go between so that my soul could tell him what I needed to learn in order to be able to communicate directly with it. Her description of what was happening actually hit a string with me as years earlier I had been told that the soul was like the driver of a vehicle and the vehicle was your physical body, so in that sense I was able to rationalise what she had just told me.

She went on to explain to me how I could train myself to listen to my body and thus my soul and said that I should really try to attune to a higher frequency in order to achieve this.

Although I did not quite understand exactly how to do this, I instinctively knew what was required. I sat that in the back of my mind and asked her another question. What really is my role in all of this? She looked at me and replied, I really can't tell you that Ron, but I am sure it will be revealed to you when the time is right. I considered what she had said and realised that when I looked back, it had indeed all been in the timing that events in the past had happened. I had not realised it before but at that instant when I looked back over my life all of the significant events in my life seemed to be illuminated and corresponded with another event which in turn made all of these events tell a story. It all seemed to fit together like a jigsaw puzzle, and it was at that point that I realised that in order to go forward, you must look back. I have done these many times since and it always gives me a clear and concise view of the progress I have made and the changes I had made in my life to get there, whether I realised it at the time or not.

Over the next 10 weeks, I learnt a new lesson every week and always achieved the desired results in that timeframe. I kept a dream journal at Darleena's request, as she told me that all of the new experiences, I was experiencing would now wash over into my sleep time and I may have some really powerful dreams, so I needed to record them. Keep the journal right next to your bed and if you have a dream, write it down as soon as you wake before you forget it. I did as I was asked and some of the dreams actually left me in awe.

Some of these lessons I undertook were designed to push me to listen to my body and intuitions more freely and without thought of what I was doing. I realised very quickly that this was in fact very helpful and always gave me a different perspective. Besides this, I quickly realised that the state I was in during my dreaming, was the same state I got into during my meditation. They were linked. I never realise it at the start, but it came to light eventually when I did a look back to go forward session.

Anyway, as I was saying earlier, in some of the later sessions Darleena would tell me to ask my body where it would like to have today's lesson. My mind's eye always took me back to one of several spots at Mitimiti and then the guided meditation would run its course at that place. It was a really beautiful, peaceful and enlightening experience and as I was familiar with my surroundings, I felt safe and protected. I innately knew I was not only being reunited with my spiritual background but also my spiritual self and spiritual home. This had been the very essence of the training I was being taught.

It was one of the most enlightening and powerful sequences of events I had ever had the privilege of experiencing.

CHAPTER 12

Travelling Home

The dreams started and I am glad Darleena told me to document them as they tended to be extensions of what I was learning, almost the same function as fine tuning a TV. She was teaching me how to tune in to get reception and the dreams were doing the fine tuning. To me, that is the best way to explain how I saw it working and it did not bother me. I saw it for what it was and soaked it up like a sponge. I say dreams but realistically it was astral travel. I realised this the very first time I left my body and went through the ceiling looking down on my body that still lay in the bed.

I was taken back to Mitimiti on many occasions and told of my responsibilities and what my role was to be. The sensation of flying with no plane was amazing to experience as I was being shown what I would be responsible for. These astral travels are so real that you are actually there. That is why I have referred to some lessons as being soul-destroying, because you are actually there. Later as I was going back down through the ceiling, I noticed the alarm clock as I re-joined my body. I made a mental note to turn the alarm clock so I could see it every time I left and returned so that I knew how long I had been away for.

The following morning, I woke up and looked around the room. I remembered my dream and the mental note to move the alarm clock so I can see it. I still do it to this day and the alarm clock is still in position for that purpose.

These astral travels revealed many of the aspects of the role that I was being prepared for so much so that I want to share the following experience with you.

On this particular night, as normal, I saw my body lying on the bed and the time on my alarm clock was 1.30am as I again floated away through the ceiling. I then found myself seated in a bus travelling along the road without a clue as to where I was headed. I began looking out the windows trying to see if I recognised any landmarks, but all of the surroundings were foreign to me. The bus picked up a number of people at different bus stops and at one point I tried to exit the bus at a bus stop and found I could not move. I took this as a sign that I was to stay on the bus. I continued looking at the surroundings to see if I felt anything familiar while the bus continued to pick up people until it was almost full. As we were travelling down what looked like a main road, I suddenly became aware of the bus leaving the ground, just like the car at the end of the movie Grease. The bus lifted off the ground and began to fly like a plane getting higher and higher. At one stage I looked through the back window of the bus and I could see planet earth behind us just as you would in a spaceship.

I turned to face the front again and there was a conductor on the bus handing out what looked to be meat pies, but only certain people were receiving them. I received my pie and looked around at the others who had received one and they all just sat there holding their pies not actually doing anything with them. I looked up to the front of the bus and out through the windscreen and could not believe what I could see. We were approaching a bus stop in the middle of space, literally. The bus shelter and the bus stop sign were just floating in space anchored to absolutely nothing. The bus pulled to a stop and the doors opened with a hiss of air from the cylinders. The conductor again stood up at the front of the bus and stood in the aisle. May I have your attention please he said in a loud voice. Could all of you who have received a pie remain seated, while those of you who did not receive a pie please make your way to the front of the bus quickly and quietly and exit the bus. I am very sorry but you are not yet ready for this journey, so it is time for you to go back. I watched as almost three quarters of the people on the bus exited through the doors and I watched as they fell back to earth. The doors then closed, and the bus moved forward and continued further out into space. At this point the conductor came walking down the aisle and I called him over to my seat. Why were they sent back I asked? Don't you worry sir, they just are not ready for this journey yet and they will go away and do some work and try once more when they think they are ready again, he said. I then asked what the pie represented, and he replied, you are to eat the pie sir, it represents all of the knowledge you will ever require to complete your journey as this will be your last time here in this place, you will not be coming back. I slowly ate the pie as I looked around the bus to see the others eating their pies too. I continued eating and just as I swallowed the last mouthful the bus pulled up at what seemed to be a gatehouse. We were all asked to leave the bus and as we all assembled outside, two people approached us from the gatehouse to welcome us. They started to introduce themselves when I suddenly said, I know you. I can remember you from the last time I was here.

They came over to me and said that can't be possible because when you leave here, we erase all of your past memory. I was all excited now and responded with, when you asked me if I could remember any of my past, I said no but I tricked you. I could still remember but then you sent me off before I could tell you that is how I know who you are now. They both looked at each other and started laughing and said, He does remember us, you always were cheeky when you were here last time as well, then we all had a laugh before we were ushered away into groups.

We were told, you are going to be given a tour of this place as you each have an important lesson to learn based on what you all have already learnt. The lessons are not necessarily the same for each of you, but you will be able to discover your lesson from within the group, so stay close.

We walked in through the main gate and I immediately thought this looked like a Hollywood movie set. We walked a short distance and then turned a corner to the left. I looked up and saw my father, Atama, Uncle Tom and a number of other rangatira all standing behind a golden braided barrier rope like you see in Hotels. I ran up to them and as I got closer, I also saw Anaru Ngawaka and all of these other people behind this group of Chiefs. Many of them were not known to me but the feelings I felt as I approached, I just knew they were all my Tupuna and their numbers were many. I ran over to see my dad and Atama said to me, we are very happy to see you have accepted boy but stay with that fella as he has some very important things to show you. We can talk whenever we like but for now you need to learn what he has to show you, it will be one of the most important lessons for you to learn here. I bid them farewell and re-joined the group. I turned to wave back to dad, and he had a big smile on his face as he held his hand up in a wave. I followed our group trying to see as much as I could see. The first few exhibits did nothing for me, so I knew those lessons were not mine to learn.

We went around the next corner and I saw a bus lying on its side. I made my way to the front of the group to try to hear what the guide was saying when suddenly the spirit of a small girl floated through the still smoking bus. I asked the guide what had happened, and he replied that the girl has just passed away very quickly and had found herself in limbo. She will stay here as long as she needs until she decides to move on. Her passing was quick, so she does not understand that she has passed over. He went on to tell me that keepers can go into limbo if need be to guide these souls to the light. When I asked how they would know if souls were in limbo, he replied, keepers just know.

All of a sudden, I saw in my mind that she had jumped from the bus and was rolling over and over down the road verge. As she rolled over for the last time her head hit a rock on the side of the road, and she passed away. It was at this point I found myself in that bus with the little girl reliving the sequence of events leading up to her death. We were on the bus which was travelling down a steep country road and the bus started to speed up. I looked to the front of the bus and could see the driver struggling to control it and a vision flashed before my eyes showing that the brake lines had severed causing the loss of brakes. The driver yelled to us to get out then opened the doors and jumped out of the runaway bus. I grabbed the girl and ran to the doors, I wrapped her in my arms as tight as I could, told her to hold on to me as tight as she could, and we jumped from the bus. We rolled down the side of the road on the grass and I held on as tightly as I could, hoping I could save the little girl's life. We rolled uncontrollably before I could finally feel our bodies slowing down. I could hear the girl still screaming as I still had her tightly bundled in my arms and thought to myself, I've done it, I've done it, I have saved her life. Just as we were coming to a stop, with the last roll, one of my arms flew open and her head rolled out and hit the same rock I had seen earlier instantly killing her. I was gutted. I could not believe that I had failed to save her life; 6'3 and 128 kg and I could not save this little girl.

This was one of those soul-destroying lessons I mentioned earlier. Being so close but not being able to do what you set out to do. I went very quiet and continued to follow the group beating myself up for failing her but also for receiving the lesson I was to learn in such a manner. I noticed that all the other lessons that we were witnessing were for the others as I had already faced them in a slightly different way but enough to see I had already been there. I was still beating myself up about my lesson and still had not spoken a word to anyone since it had happened.

At the end of the tour, we were each taken aside to see if we understood the lesson we had been shown. When it was my turn the guide asked me, did you receive the lesson you were to receive? I replied that I did but I felt gutted that I was unable to help the way I had wanted to. He said to me be kind to yourself Ron, we knew you would try to do that. It is in your good heart, but did you get the lesson? I again said yes. I was asked to tell them what the lesson was but all I could think of was that little girl. With tears welling in my eyes I replied, the lesson was that I have been given a very special gift, but it does not mean I can change the future and I am not to interfere with free will. Whatever is meant to happen must happen.

The guides said to me, yes, we understand it is a very hard lesson to learn and many before you have done exactly the same as you. Your reaction to the lesson is the compassionate and empathetic side of you coming out but the most important thing is that you did actually find the lesson. Many who have faced this lesson have failed but you Ron have passed this test. They were congratulating me, but I was in no mood to celebrate. I saw a few of the others had gone quiet well so I am sure they must have also learnt their lessons.

My guide went on to explain more about this place called limbo.

He explained that there is no such thing as hell but there is a limbo which is a stopover for spirits. Limbo is for those who pass over so quickly they can't accept or believe that they have actually passed. Time is an earthly trait and does not exist here, so spirits can be here with no perception of time until they move along. The reason you were shown limbo is that you will now be able to visit limbo when you need to, as the keeper of your clan or tribe, to guide them to the light when needed. I accepted the explanation but inside I was still reeling after the experience. I told him that they could find a better way to present that lesson so that it was not so soul-destroying to which he replied, it is presented in this manner so that you do not forget the lesson or the parameters of the lesson. I had no choice but to accept that explanation.

Apart from what I described as soul-destroying lessons, I found the whole learning experience to be a very surreal and smooth flowing experience. The path taken by way of these meditations began with intensifying focus then went on to colour healing, which I might add, really does work and really well. From here we went on to reconnecting with the worlds' energy and the following session was in fact to connect with mother earth herself. This would have had to have been one of the most emotional and powerful spiritual experiences I have ever had the privilege of being a part of.

I did keep a journal of these events but as time went on, I relied on my memory as I found that all I had to do was think of it and it would once again fill my thoughts in detail. I quite often look back at what I had written in the few records I still have and am instantly transported back to relive that same experience and each time, I come out of the experience with something else that I have learnt. I found that as I was ready for certain information or knowledge, it would reveal itself to me and I would take it on board.

As I had found all along this journey, the universe reveals what you need as you need it, you can't force it. It is a seemingly pre-determined journey whereas the information you need along the way is revealed to you at the right time. You just have to tune in and be open to the universe and the knowledge it has to offer. The ultimate goal of all this knowledge is to reconnect with your higher self and it is truly a beautiful and emotional experience. It has unlocked many emotions and thoughts that I never thought I would be possible of harbouring and, to be very honest, the euphoric sensations and feelings I have experienced on many occasions would be the best experiences I have had in my life, bar none.

I will not go into the rest of the training sessions we did but I did ask Darleena one day how she knew exactly what I needed from one week to the next as it was virtually seamless in as much as that it just flowed like a river.

She said that the three gentlemen that were with me constantly were telling her exactly what to show me from one week to the next. It was as if they already had it planned for me and were just waiting for me to accept it.

I began looking forward to my final "test" each week with Atama as it was a challenge to me on a weekly basis, to show I had learnt the lesson which was tasked of me to learn.

At the conclusion of the ten weeks it took me to learn all of my lessons, Darleena sat down with me at the end of the final lesson and told me that she had been told to tell me that I had done better than expected and they were proud of what I had achieved. She then went on to say that from her own perspective, she had never seen anyone go through that much training at such an intense rate and come out the other side of it like a ball of energy. You were more than ready for this Ron. No wonder they chose you she said. You were just a very heavy sleeper that they found hard to awaken.

We said our farewells and I headed off home quite happy with what I had achieved yet finding myself in a void. What is next I thought to myself on the way home. I picked Brett up from school and we went home and took our bikes out for a ride while his mum was still working in her shop.

About an hour later I went home and started dinner while Brett stayed out with his mates and Leanne was still finishing up in the shop.

I had this really strange feeling like I had lost my best friend and for the life of me I just could not figure out why. We had dinner and were sitting outside having a cup of coffee when I turned to Leanne and said, I have got to go do a meditation, something is not sitting right with me.

I went into my space and set up to meditate but as I turned to go and turn the lights off, Atama was already behind the candle once more with the lights still on.

I sat in my chair and straight away noticed a different feel to the energy in the room. Then from behind Atama came my father and Uncle Tom. They had come to say goodbye.

In the beginning they told me that they had three months to spend with me to show me what they needed to show me. I had exceeded expectations and finished with time in hand. Now they had completed their task, it was time to leave.

Again, they praised my efforts during the training and told me to keep practicing all I had learnt because I would need it all in the future. They then said that if I wanted to learn more, I would need to move home to Mitimiti and that I would know when the time was right.

I said a karakia and closed the session. I went back out to the lounge and told Leanne what had happened. She gave me a hug and Brett came and gave me a big hug and said, it will be alright dad. It was so cute and put a big smile on my face.

Back to being on my own again but at least this time, I felt alive.

CHAPTER 13

Get Down to Business

I carried on with the sessions on my own and if I needed any guidance a quick call to Darleena was all that was required. I had this.

I got very good practice and started incorporating many of my practices into the work I was doing in Perth on a waste to energy project which as it turned out, was way ahead of its time.

My belief is that if you have the right intent you are able to use your skills to help with bringing these benefits into existence.

I found that I was able to use some of my newfound abilities to assist me in achieving the goals set in order to get the facility through the licensing phase.

For example, during the public consultation phase, I found that I could look out over the crowd and tell by the colour of their aura's who supported the proposal and who did not. I never tried to make it happen, it just happened as I was in tune. I could then focus on those people that were not convinced and walk them through a complete presentation having them understand and support the entire proposal by the end of the night. It became a methodology I would use from here on in as it enabled me to identify problems almost immediately upon entering these venues. My intent in this project had always been positive and environmentally driven and I believed that if the intent is for the greater good then I would be justified in using my skills to a certain degree.

At this stage I had no experience in public speaking or spear heading a 740m waste to energy project, but I found I was being taught and led by my guides. This is going to sound weird but at times I felt myself being sucked into the void behind my eyes and another presence entering that space and taking over. I had no fear and found that all the knowledge that was required to carry off such a task just flowed from my tongue with conviction and confidence.

I remember presenting to the Shadow Ministry in Government House in Perth. In a pre-presentation chat with the leader of the Shadow Ministry and three ministers, I was being grilled about where I was from, my career background and how I got involved with the project etc.

I explained I was a Maori living in Kalgoorlie with a diverse background covering many industries and, on that basis, had been engaged as a Project Manager for this particular overseas company behind the proposal to represent them in Western Australia. As soon as I said I had been in WA for almost 20 years, I was told, and I quote 'Well you have been here long enough to call you one of ours' unquote. With that said it was down to business.

There was a constant stream of pollies coming into the State Room as we were setting up our presentation and I was really beginning to get quite nervous until I was informed when all were present.

I looked over at Ian Dryden (ran operations in Perth while I was in Kalgoorlie) who looked very nervous, but he told me the video presentation was good to go. I told him to start the video then turned to face the crowd which numbered in excess of 30 shadow ministry members. That in itself was quite intimidating and out of nowhere I suddenly came out with an ice breaker. With my back to the large video screen I looked around the crowd, introduced myself and the company I was representing and welcomed them to our video presentation and project introduction. I looked around the room and saw everyone was focussed on what I was presenting, then without thinking I just said to the room 'If you see three big XXXs come up on the screen, please feel free to give me a discrete nod and I will get the video changed; it will be the wrong one'.

The room just erupted in laughter and one of the ministers I had spoken with earlier said in a loud voice, 'you have definitely come up from Kalgoorlie' and again the room erupted in laughter.

From here on in the ice was broken, the stuffiness dissipated, and the presentation went on without a hitch. At the completion of the presentation we were quite surprised by the number of shadow ministers that came up to us and gave their cards and offered support to us in order to see if we couldn't 'get this bird in the air' was one phrase used.

We actually received a lot of support from both sides of Parliament which was reflected in a 3.5-year licensing timeframe rather than the 15-year timeline that the Environmental Protection Agency (EPA) had envisaged.

During that timeline of 3.5 years, there were a number of occasions where we had hit brick walls which required me to again ask for help. I would go to bed at night exhausted and ask for help to solve the issues we were facing. Each time I would receive the answers in my dreams at around 1 to 2 am. As I was used to using a dream journal, I was still in the habit of keeping a book and pen next to the bed. I would get up and write it all down word for word, while it was fresh in my head. Then I would type it all up and make as many copies as we needed and by 6am we would be having breakfast discussing the new plan we were undertaking to navigate the brick wall. This method never let us down once and to me it was a strengthening of faith, Trust and Acceptance of my spirituality.

On one particular occasion, I failed to understand what was being told to me and I could not see how it would fit into the framework we were operating within. I never told the others, but I did say a little prayer, then looked up and said I do not understand how this is supposed to help us, but you have not let me down yet, so I presented the plan to the team and we rolled with it. Not understanding it, just implementing it as asked. The amazing results spoke for themselves.

I realised that I do not have to understand everything I was being told. My guides were working for the best outcome even if I couldn't see it from my viewpoint. That was a huge thing for me to discover and is the reason I say sometimes you have to look back in order to go forward. I never understood how it was supposed to work but when I looked back, in hindsight I saw that if it was not actioned as I was shown, then the flow on effects would not have occurred, thus making the entire situation work as it was originally intended. This journey had just given me another lesson I was not to forget and one that has happened on many occasions since.

On one of these occasions, I had flown into Perth from Kalgoorlie and a friend of ours who had moved to Perth with her partner and kids, called me to see if I had enough time to catch up with her before I flew back to the goldfields. She had been to see Chanty in Perth and was wondering if I could just listen to the tape as she had recorded the reading. The four days that I had been in Perth working on the project was hectic and on the final day I never got back to the motel till 7pm.

Our friend lived about twenty mins from the motel so I called her and told her I would shower and head over. She told me she had made dinner and not to eat at the motel.

I never got to their house until 9pm. I had already packed my bags as I had to be at the airport at 6am but had an overnight bag with a change for the next day. I did not get to see the girls as it was too late for them to be up and her partner was out of town for work.

She gave me a beautiful dinner and then we sat in the lounge and she began telling me about her reading. She explained she could hear murmuring in the background of the recording and just wanted me to listen to it and see what I thought. I was sitting at one end of a sofa leaning on an armrest when she went to put the cassette into the stereo. As she was coming back to take a seat, I just opened my hand that was on the armrest and asked her to sit on the floor and lean back so the nape of her neck rested in the crook of my hand.

As we waited for the recording to start, I just relaxed and prepared myself as I would normally do in order to meditate.

The recording started playing and I could hear Chanty talking to our friend prior to the reading taking place. The reading began after a few seconds and things went as normal for the first few minutes. As the reading progressed, the video in my mind started up and the story of my friend's life played before me like a movie in a cinema. I lived through her whole life feeling every emotion as if she had felt it, the ups the downs, the extreme highs and then the depths of despair. It was while I was in the depths of despair of her life that I discovered a secret. It was by no means a small secret, it was huge and had me crying like a blithering idiot, not something many people had ever seen me do. I could not move until the movie screen in my mind had stopped rolling. It stopped at the same time as the tape recording which was a 30 min recording. It was not until the recording of the reading stopped that I found myself in darkness as the movie screen in my mind had gone blank.

I worked toward bringing myself out of this place. I did not want to stay there. It did take a while as my friend thought I had gone to sleep.

When I came back, I started to move my hands and she got

up to turn around to see tears still streaming down my face. She asked me what was wrong, and I started profusely apologising to her saying I was so, so, sorry I never mean to. 'You never meant to what' she said looking at me with a puzzled frown. I tried to regain some composure and quietly said to her, 'I feel I have ripped open your chest and exposed your soul without asking your permission and now I know your secret'.

She didn't say anything, she just glared at me. Finally, she said, 'what secret'? to which I replied, 'your dad'.

There was a sullen silence which was only momentary, then she started to sob and then cry. I hugged her and again apologised to which there was no reply. I felt absolutely terrible. I could still feel the residual energy from that experience in my body so I told her I would be back shortly and went outside to find a large tree to ground myself.

By this time, it would have been close to midnight as I am walking the neighbourhood looking for the largest tree I could find. The neighbours would have spun out if they had seen me. It took a while, but I found a huge tree only a few houses down the road and it was on the front of the property, so I proceeded to hug the tree and ask it to take all of the residual energy and any negativity from me and return it to the earth.

Once I had done this I went back to the house and she was still sitting in the same chair just staring blankly at nothing.

Again, I said I was sorry. She just motioned for me to sit down and then she just started to tell me what had happened to her when she was younger. She had blocked it out a long time ago. I will not go into details, but her parents finally split up and she went to live with her mum and her new partner and had managed to bury those memories deep within herself. Unfortunately, I had dug them up again without even trying.

I remember her brothers telling me that when they were young and their sister left with mum and her new partner, they would run outside every day to see if mum had come back for them, but she never came. When they were older, they left New Zealand and tracked down their mum, sister and now stepdad who were living in Tasmania at the time. Later on, they all moved to Western Australia for work and that is where our paths crossed.

We stayed up talking for the remainder of the night until I had to leave for the airport. I mean after what had happened, I couldn't just say ok well I am off to bed catch you later bye. When it was time for me to head to the airport I again apologised and by this time, she had calmed down and come to terms with what had happened. She said to me 'I think it is time I talked to my dad'.

I still felt terrible and when I left, I gave her a huge hug and told her if she needed support she knew where to find us.

I headed off to the airport, returned the hire car and boarded my flight back to Kalgoorlie.

I got home that morning totally exhausted. When I got home

Leanne and Brett were both up and breakfast was just hitting the table. Brett was so excited to see me he was all over me telling me what he wanted to do at the local fair. I had forgotten it was on, but I was not going to let him down, so we had breakfast, then I had a shower and a coffee then we headed off to the fair.

I never had a chance to talk to Leanne about what had transpired the previous night until Brett was enjoying rides and running around with his mates at the fair. She took it on board with a look of concern and said she would call our friend during the week. I could hardly keep my eyes open for the rest of the day and managed to sneak 40 winks here and there from behind the dark sunglasses I was wearing.

When we finally got home at around 3pm, I showered and then went to bed where I slept until the next morning.

The next day, I woke up still feeling under a cloud of guilt. During the course of the day and the following day too for that matter, I tried to shake it off but to no avail.

On the third day I really needed some help so I called Darleena and told her I would be in town the following day if she could fit me in. We set a time and then I just collapsed in bed feeling terrible and eventually fell asleep.

The following morning, I awoke still feeling flat as if I was hungover even though I know I was not. I thought I would try to meditate before heading into town to see Darleena but try as I might,

I just could not do it. All that happened was I went straight to sleep. I woke up again about 30 to 40 mins later and was so frustrated with my result.

I decided to take a quick shower and then had a coffee and toast for breakfast.

Leanne had already taken Brett to school and had a client in her hair salon, so I just popped my head in the door to tell her I was off to town. She came outside to make sure I was ok and even offered to drive me in to town after finishing her client, but I told her I would be ok, and we would chat when I got home.

I headed into Kalgoorlie and stopped in for my appointment with Darleena. She asked me what was wrong as she said my normal demeanour was amiss today.

After she held the door open for my entourage, I sat down and said to her that something had happened that I needed to talk with her about.

I proceeded to tell her of the events that happened when I visited our friend in Perth. I explained how I felt I had ripped her chest open and seen the very essence of her soul while living and feeling every experience and every emotion that she had ever experienced in her whole lifetime. I had experienced the same depths of despair, the same highs of euphoria and the same feelings of contentedness that this woman had felt in her entire life. Her whole life had been shown to me in minutes. I then told her of the secret I had inadvertently uncovered. I was a total wreck trying to convey all of this information to Darleena.

We sat for a few minutes in silence with me feeling like a train wreck, when Darleena cleared her throat before speaking. You know Ron, I know the training you did was very intense over a very short period of time but that was not the end of your training, she said.

Those men that were here for your mentoring have very powerful energies and I think I have told you before I have never seen an energy like that on its own let alone three separate energies all focussing on the same student. All I can suggest is that you be very careful with intent because your energy is also getting more powerful as you discover more, and I do not really know where your boundaries are. It's as if you just have to try something and you can do it. You have experienced rebirthing without even trying really. I sat and thought about what she had just said. I made a mental note to ensure intent was always for positive things and not negative and told myself to never forget that note. You need to constantly be aware of what you are putting out there and that you are fully aware of your intent. This gift you have been given is very powerful so I can't tell you what you can or can't do, you will hopefully find that out along the way, she said, but with what you have shown us all during your training, you will be fine.

I left Darleena with her telling me that they had chosen me for many reasons and one of them was the pure heart which she said was how she knew I would always have the right intent with anything I explored.

We hugged and I headed home.

CHAPTER 14

The Move

For the next few months things were relatively quiet. I kept practicing meditation and all the lessons I had learnt. My workload meant I was still flying back and forward to Perth every 4 days. I carried on as normal and then one day out of the blue Leanne and I started talking about moving to Perth. Friends of ours were interested in renting our house in Coolgardie. We wanted Brett to have the best chance of a decent education as the reputation of the local Primary School wasn't very good.

We decided to take the jump and move to Perth. We packed up the house and Leanne had a closing down party for the business and we were off. I hired a truck from Perth and my cousin Gerry, and his mate Greg drove it the 575 kms out from Perth to our place. I had the entire house packed up and stacked into the garage so that when the truck arrived, we just had to reverse it up to the garage, load the truck and head straight to Perth. I had also hired a storage unit in Perth to store our furniture until we got a place. In the short term we would be staying with cousins Gerry and Rachel Te Toko.

It did not take long to find a place. Meanwhile I was still travelling backward and forward from Kalgoorlie to Perth. I really did not want to be away from the family again but for us to be in Perth and do what we needed to do, that was what it was going to take.

I had been keeping up with my meditations all this time and had begun to lose interest. It felt like the lessons I had learnt had merely expanded my box of consciousness to a larger box. I again felt trapped and it was beginning to frustrate me. I had learnt all the lessons and honed my skills and found that I could use each one of them without even trying. I was truly connected but I still felt something was missing.

As we all know, things happen for a reason. Even if the occurrence seems bad, it happens so that you can learn an important lesson. In this particular instance an accident gave me the time and opportunity to learn the biggest lesson to date.

As I said earlier, I was still travelling back and forward between Perth and Kalgoorlie. While I was in Kalgoorlie, I stayed with my brother Harry and Janice and their family. Due to the fact that I was doing 12-hour days, my time in Kalgoorlie was strictly work eat and sleep for 4 days then head back to Perth, put on a suit and represent the project.

It was during one of these swings that the following event took place.

I was underground at work this particular night, when I was using a hand crane to lift ground control materials onto the back of a Ute to be taken to the face at the start of the shift. I was lifting one end of multiple sheets of mesh on our work Ute when the brake locking mechanism failed. I had let go of the handle after lifting mesh to tie to the side of the vehicle when the handle then spun out of control hitting the back of my hand with an almighty crack. As it turned out, after visiting the hospital, the carpels were fractured on the back of my right hand.

The safety office did not want a lost time incident, so I was put on light duties.

I was flown back and forward to Perth at the company's expense for the entire time I was on light duties. The company also provided transport so that I was picked up every morning from my brother's and taken to work by one of the office girls. Once at work I would go to the prestart meeting, sign on and chat with my crew. Once they went down the hole to work, I would sign off and the same office girl would run me back to town. My daily routine took 3 hours max and the rest of the day was mine.

My next opportunity came to me during this time while reading the local newspaper the Kalgoorlie Miner. I came across an advertisement that read, Group Meditation for all levels. It was being run by one of the local stores called The Crystal Den. The Crystal Den was a local shop that stocked many items among them crystals, spiritual books, music, incense sage and many other items used by spiritual practitioners and students. I had been there to purchase a candle for my training.

I had tried a few other meditation groups in Perth on trips home, Buddhist, eastern and western meditation styles but none had interested me. I walked out of all of them. They were all religion based and that never sat well with me for reasons I will not go on to explain.

I considered it for a while and thought to myself, maybe I am meant to go. Maybe this is more than coincidence that I now had the time with my current work situation to attend. I decided I would go along. The following night was a Wednesday and I went along to the venue to see what it was like. I told my sister in law Janice about it and she came along as well.

There was a small crowd of about twelve people including myself. It was quite a good size room above one of the shops in the main street near Monty's which used to be near the top of town.

I introduced myself to the women organising the group and met the other attendees prior to the class starting. There was a good mix of ages in the group as well as a mix of genders, so it turned out to be quite a balanced and diverse group of people.

At the beginning of the class we all had to stand, say who we were and what we were hoping to learn. I gave my name but was quite guarded about what I hoped to learn as I did not know anyone personally or their stories. I said enough to keep them happy but not enough to know where I was, if you know what I mean.

Once we had all introduced ourselves, we were asked to stand and form a circle. The sound of a single beating drum filled the room. Its sound bounced off of the walls loud and clear. We were then told that we would be doing the ohm meditation which works on vibration. I had been introduced to this at a previous meditation that I had walked out on, so I was in two minds but decided to give it a go as the energy in the room felt good.

I began the ohm meditation and a few minutes later I thought to myself this is not doing anything for me. I think I was questioning whether I would get anything out of this when the teacher spoke. I want you to all join hands in the circle. I remember thinking to myself, really? I held my hands out to my sides to join with the people either side of me. The results were instant. I tapped into the energy of the others in the circle. They were open, they were here, and they were giving me a boost with their collective energy. The video screen in my mind came into view and I saw myself strapped into a seat as a crash test dummy. I am sitting in the seat looking straight ahead then suddenly the brake trips and I am launched toward a brick wall at breakneck speed. As I am launching down the rails, I hear a voice in my mind. The voice says to me are you going to save yourself and jump or are you going to hang on for the ride and see what happens. As always, the choice is yours the voice said. The adrenaline was pumping, and my hands were gripping the seat in which I was strapped. I only had a split second to think and by now I could clearly see the grout between the bricks. I made my choice in that split second and gripped the chair I was seated in even harder, rolled my shoulders in and said with my inner voice, bring it on.

A millisecond later I squinted my eyes as I hit the brick wall with full force. I was amazed when I hit the wall because what I felt was not the splat that I was expecting but rather the feeling of being light as a feather along with the sensation of flying. I fully opened my eyes and found myself floating and flying among the stars. I looked back to where I had come from and saw the hole in the brick wall through which I had come. I turned forward again to enjoy the sensation of flying and realised that I had found my home. I was back to be a part of the universe. Atama, my father and my Uncle Tom had prepared me for this journey. They had shown me what I would need and sent me on my way. I now felt complete and for the very first time in my life I felt I belonged.

I could still hear everything that was going on in the meditation, but I kept floating and flying in the universe until the teacher said it was time to leave where we were and return to the room. I gently floated back into myself in the room and followed the teacher's prompts, up till she told us all to open our eyes and then I slowly opened my eyes and I was back in the room, back in the circle.

I still felt like I was as light as a feather, I felt energised, I felt amazing. We were all asked to share something from our experience and when it came to my turn to contribute, I proceeded to tell of my experience. After everyone had shared their experiences, a prayer was offered, and the hour-long session was over. We were all helping to clean up the room when the teacher said she would be going over the road to Monty's diner for a cup of tea if anyone would care to join her and discuss anything. I was not planning on sharing anything any further but decided I would go over for a coffee. I went on over, ordered a coffee and sat down at a table. A few of the others joined me but some just got a takeaway coffee and had to leave. The teacher joined us at the table and others had engaged her in conversation about that night's session. I really wasn't listening to what was being said as I was still charged and could feel energy all over my body. I was just taking it all in, enjoying the energy and the euphoria of it all. I had never felt so alive as I did right then, it was amazing. Eventually there were just four of us left at the table. Two had begun a private conversation when the teacher turned to me and said in almost a whisper, 'what really happened with you. I looked over at you and I swear you were floating above the floor and your aura is so much brighter than when you arrived at the session'. I started telling her what had happened when we were interrupted by the last two from the group saying their goodbyes and heading home. We bid them farewell ordered another coffee each and returned to our conversation. She asked me if that night's experience held any significance for me. I thought for a while and answered her, 'yes it did'. I explained to her what 'that night's event meant to me. I told her that I had begun a journey and found myself locked inside of a larger box than I had started with. I couldn't figure out how to break free from that box but through a series of recent circumstances, I had found myself in her meditation class that evening.

I did not know what to expect and told her how I had walked out of other meditation classes but the energy from this group felt good or even comfortable, so I stayed. I told her of the energy and events of what happened after I linked hands with the circle. I explained how I had felt trapped inside of a box and tonight the universe had shown me how to break out of that box. There will be no more boxes for me to exist in.

This was just one of the many mind-blowing examples that I have been lucky enough to experience on my journey. On your journey you will understand what I mean when you are lucky enough to have experienced something so powerful beautiful and totally orgasmic. When you do, I want you to remember the feeling, it will become addictive.

The teacher sat in silence for a few minutes then looked at me and said she felt that she could no longer take the class, that it should be me. I quietly said to her, we all have our part to play. I am not the teacher that is your role. I am trying to find my way on my journey, and you helped me by giving me the tools and helping me to take the next step. That is what all of us travellers do for each other, either I have something for you or vice versa, even if we do not know it at the time. I said, you had something for me tonight and for that I thank you sincerely. This is all normal when you are on your journey.

She told me that seeing stuff like this in her classes was very rare, but she felt like it gives her something to focus on now, along with validation that the attraction of like-minded people really does work. In this case we both got something out of it which is a good thing. I continued to go for the following two weeks and every guided meditation she put us into, I continued to feel the power and all-encompassing love of the white light.

After the last session I attended, the group again went to

Monty's diner afterwards for a coffee, tea or whatever. I told the teacher I probably would not be back from here on in as my medical clearance should be issued in the next few days, meaning I would go back onto roster and would not have the time to attend, as well as the fact I was now living in Perth. I thanked her for facilitating what I needed to move forward. We hugged and she said that if someone had told her this story and that she would be part of it, she would have told them it would never happen. Now that it has happened, she said it had sparked something inside her so now she also wanted to take that step and was going to refocus on her own personal growth.

From my own perspective, I now know that I am part of the universe and with the help of my Tupuna, they will continue to guide me and lead me to where I need to be in order that I achieve what I have set out to do. I have at times said I did not agree with the way some of the lessons have been presented but when you get what you have asked for, I suppose you can't really argue. If I had not fractured my carpel, the series of events as explained in this story would never have happened, so the end result would never have happened in this timeframe. I knew my Tupuna were helping me because I could feel their familiar energy's when I needed to.

I had been bought into a place where I could tap into other people's energy in order to allow me to break out of my box and reconnect with the universe. I felt completely at ease with the situation and the teacher was thankful to have been a huge part of my growth. I am now ready for what lies ahead. I just do not know what it is yet.

In saying that, my journey so far has spanned 47 years as of Easter Sunday 2020. I was working on this book on the Saturday afternoon when I realised it so rather than working on into the night like I have been doing for months, I stopped working at 7pm, relaxed had a nice dinner of snapper and chips with a few sausages for Gypsy my dog (her favourite treat) and then at 9pm which is 1 am New Zealand time, I recited a Karakia and made a toast to our Tupuna. Now with the knowledge they have entrusted to me, I move forward with a spring in my step knowing I have something to complete in this lifetime, all the while knowing they are walking alongside me guiding and encouraging me. I know that there are others in our hapu and Iwi that are like me, I used to hear stories when I was growing up, and I am reaching out to these people to let them know you are not alone, and I am here to help. All you have to do is ask. I have been where you are now, I have felt what you have felt, I have seen what you have seen. This journey of mine is not about me. It is about all of us as a collective race of people whose spiritual belonging spans back more than the 1050 years when Kupe landed on these shores. It is your birthright should you choose to discover it. These spiritual journeys have been taken by our people for many, many, generations and we have all heard the stories that have been passed down from our Tupuna. When I look back at my own life, I see the scared 7-year- old boy, the out of control teenager and even the wild twenty something year old. I embrace them and hold on to their memory because they were all the vehicles I used to get to here. I am proud of my heritage and I for one don't want to forget who I am or where I have come from again. Never stop telling

223

the stories of our people, our Tupuna do not want us to forget them either.

You may be wondering why I have a karakia at the front and the back of the book. Originally, I was only going to tell my story and I didn't really know how I was going to approach it. After starting the book seven times I finally decided in which angle I was going to approach it which is what you have read. Anyway, it was only a month ago I decided to include a synopsis of both rangatira in order to illustrate who they were. Thanks to cousin Jaqi Brown the great, great, great granddaughter of Anaru Ngawaka and awesome keeper of stories and whanau records for providing his synopsis.

I compiled the synopsis on Atama and done my own synopsis on Anaru which I sent to Jaqi to review. I inserted both my versions into the document so I could format the book while waiting to hear back from Jaqi. That night I was visited by both rangatira who told me, if you are going to do it that way, do it properly boy with karakia. So, they led me to the selected karakia, and they have been in the book ever since.

Ka Kite

Footnote

During the course of my journey I was told we had all signed a contract before we came here to achieve something in our lifetime. Chanty had once told me that as we are all on different levels our tasks are matched to where we are and where we are going. With all that I have personally experienced and been shown as well as the ongoing protection and guidance I have been the subject of as a result of my journey I have reached the conclusion that I now agree with her viewpoint. It is all food for thought and something for you to consider should you find the courage and dedication to undertake your own journey.

Epilogue

My journey has spanned all but 7 years of my life so far and began the first time that I was ever reintroduced to our spiritual home of Mitimiti. When I talk about the farm, to me it is much more than just a farm it is our connection to our past as is the entire area of the Hokianga.

My journey has allowed me to reconnect to heritage and my culture in a way in which I never dreamt of but, on reflection, in a way that I am so thankful to have bestowed upon me. My journey has exceeded my wildest expectations and has allowed me to experience the unbelievably euphoric experiences spirituality brings which I never would have discovered on my own. My understanding of Tupuna and spirituality has gone from being one based on fear to one that now knows no fear but encompasses light, compassion, empathy and most importantly love. I thank my Tupuna for guiding me and gifting me the knowledge and understanding that I have now embraced in order to reconnect with my higher self. Finally, I would like to thank you for allowing me to remain as me, as I was never wanting to lose sight of the me that began this journey. The me that started this journey serves as my anchor and gives me a sense of just how far this Waka called life has taken me.

The title of the book 'Walking with Chiefs' reflects how I personally experienced my journey and how I have been influenced by both Atama Paparangi and Anaru Ngawaka, both powerful rangatira in their own right even though ultimately I could only be mentored by one. I am still travelling on my journey and will at a later date continue with this story and what I have discovered and achieved along the way. This book covers a timespan which dates from Easter Sunday Morning in 1973 until March 1998. Much more has happened since I found myself reconnected to the universe and I am still revelling in all the new discoveries I have found along the way.

If you are at a place in your life where you are where I was, ask your body the questions and listen. If it is your time to embark on your journey your body will let you know, and it will come from within. If you are unfamiliar with your past, research it and take the first step in reconnecting with it.

I hope that some of the experiences I described have shed some light on what you are experiencing. If you find that you need to use some of what I have described to help you to move on from where you are, be my guest. That is the intention of this book, to help others. Use it as often as you need to help with what you need.

Just remember to relax, let go and trust and do not be afraid to tell your story. It may be the key to unlock someone else's prison. You are not alone on your journey; you just need to learn how to recognise the rest of us and be open so that we can recognise you.

If you require some reading material, I can suggest you read the following books, they may not give you all the answers, but more importantly they release your mind from your existing life so that it can assimilate and prepare for the new life it wishes to pursue.

The Celestine Prophecy	James Redfield
The Eagle and the Rose	Dorothy Altea
Walking in Light	Kelvin Cruikshank

New Zealand's own Kelvin Cruickshank's series of books are a good read and related to his experiences in New Zealand so be sure to give them a try. You may remember him from Sensing Murder on TV in New Zealand. I personally have never seen the series but was given one of the books by my sister Georgina who told me that after reading that particular book she related it to me, as over the years I had told her bits and pieces about where I was and what I was facing. After reading that one book I purchased the rest of the series and read them all. It was nice to know I was not the only one experiencing all of this and how he had accepted from an early age.

Reading these types of books allows your mind to slowly awaken and prepare itself for transition and that transition will take place when you awaken.

I found I could relate to all of these books through the course of my journey and it did actually let me know that I was not alone on my quest. I found that this was all I needed when things started to get me down and I was finding the road a bit hard and lonely.

I hope that they will do the same for you and make your journey a smooth path.

Walk in Love and Light

Ron Kendall

Karakia (Prayer)

Kia hora te marino

Kia whakapapa pounamu Te Moana

Hei huarahi mā tātou i te rangi nei

Aroha atu, aroha mai

Tātou i a tātou katoa

Hui e! Tāiki e!

May peace be widespread

May the sea be like greenstone

A pathway for us all this day

Let us show respect for each other

For one another

Bind us all together

Walking with Chiefs.com

walkingwithchiefs@gmail.com